CW01395760

New Perspectives and Royal & Derngate, Northampton
present

# (the)
# Woman

## by Jane Upton

(*the*) *Woman* was first performed at Royal and Derngate,
Northampton on 13 February 2025

# ≥PERSPECTIVES

| | |
|---|---|
| Artistic Director/CEO | Angharad Jones |
| Executive Director | Sally Anne Tye |

New Perspectives is the leading touring theatre company in the East Midlands with 50 years' experience of touring high-quality productions to venues of all sizes across the UK, from mid-scale theatres to village halls. With a strong rural core, they create productions to fit spaces of any size in order to bring new work that is unexpected and thought-provoking to a wide range of audiences. New Perspectives co-produced with Fifth Word a tour of *We Need New Names*, based on the Booker Prize-nominated novel, and in Autumn the company undertook a major rural tour of *Make Good – the Post Office Scandal Musical* in a co-production with Pentabus, marking the Golden anniversary of each company. As Artistic Director/CEO since 2021, Angharad Jones has directed touring productions *The Great Almighty Gill* (Edinburgh Festival & UK Tour, 2022), *The Swearing Jar* (rural/Studio UK tour, 2023) and *Model Village* (rural tour, 2023), and a script-in-hand reading of Lucy Kirkwood's *Maryland.* New Perspectives run a talent development programme, New Associates, and work with people who don't identify as artists to support them to tell their own story through their Open Pitch programme.

**www.newperspectives.co.uk**

New Perspectives is supported using public funding by Arts Council England. Registered Charity No: 1058309

Supported by
**ARTS COUNCIL ENGLAND**

# ROYAL & DERNGATE NORTHAMPTON

| | |
|---|---|
| Chief Executive | Jo Gordon |
| Artistic Director | Jesse Jones |
| Deputy CEO | |
| (Producing and Programming) | Holly Gladwell |

Royal & Derngate is proud of its reputation as a thriving regional theatre. An important entertainment hub for all communities across Northamptonshire and beyond, the three-stage and cinema complex is home to an acclaimed Made In Northampton self-produced programme as well as welcoming some of the most well-known acts and shows touring the UK. In recent years the venue has celebrated Stage, Olivier and Academy Awards nominations, notably including a prestigious win for Best Family Show at the 2020 Olivier Awards. As important as the work on its stages, its nationally recognised Creative Engagement programme works with schools, families and communities, and the Generate development programme supports hundreds of regional artists each year, at all stages of their careers.

**www.royalandderngate.co.uk**

# (the) Woman
## by Jane Upton

## Cast

*in order of appearance*

Lizzy Watts
Cian Barry
André Squire
Jamie-Rose Monk

## Creatives

| | |
|---|---|
| Dramaturg | Sarah Dickenson |
| Director | Angharad Jones |
| Designer | Sara Perks |
| Lighting Designer | Lily Woodford |
| Sound Designer | Bella Kear |
| Projection Design | Matt Powell |
| Associate Projection Designer | Farah Ishaq |
| Movement Director | Lucy Glassbrook |
| Assistant Director | Jessy Roberts |
| Casting | Ellie Collyer-Bristow CDG |

| | |
|---|---|
| Production Photography | Manuel Harlan |
| Rehearsal Photography | Tom Platinum Morley |
| Filming | Karl Poyzer |
| Image Design | Steph Pyne |
| Photography | Gemma Poyzer |

Scenery, set painting, properties, costuming, wigs and make-up by Royal & Derngate workshops and facilitated by in-house stage management and technical teams.

Thanks to Jesse Jones and the fantastic team at Royal & Derngate, Northampton, the National Theatre Generate Programme and to Archie Backhouse, Fanta Barrie, Jessica Clark, Ray Fearon, Akiya Henry, Jennifer Jackson, Sabrina Sandhu, Joe Wiltshire Smith, Jay Taylor, Jason Williamson, Rosie Wyatt for contributing to the development of the play. Special thanks to Peggy Morgan Grahame, voice of M's daughter.

# Cast

## Lizzy Watts | M

Lizzy Watts trained at The Royal Welsh College of Music and Drama.

Theatre credits include: *The Commotion Time* (Exeter Northcott); *SHED: Exploded View* (Royal Exchange, Manchester); *Either* and *Ravenscourt* (Hampstead Theatre); *Dealing With Clair* and *The False Servant* (Orange Tree); *Hedda Gabler* (National Theatre); *Strife* (Chichester Festival Theatre); *Angry Brigade* and *Artefacts* (The Bush); *God of Chaos* and *Merit* (Theatre Royal Plymouth); *A Midsummer Night's Dream* (Shakespeare's Globe); *Blink* (Nabokov); *Twelfth Night* (Filter); *Wasted* (Paines Plough).

TV credits include: *Call The Midwife, Professor T, Endeavour, The Durrells, Midsomer Murders*. Film includes: *The Best Man*.

Lizzy has recorded many radio dramas for the BBC and played regular character Ivy Layton in Radio 4's *Home Front*.

## Cian Barry | Matt, Josh and Joe

Cian Barry appeared as Heinrich Wieschhoff in Per Fly's new feature, *Hammarskjöld*, opposite *Sex Education*'s Mikael Persbrandt.

Cian has just filmed *FBI: International* and can be seen in ITV's returning crime series *DI Ray*, playing Ethan Henderson.

Further film credits include: *Falling Into Place* (Weydemann Bros.); *Snap Shot* (Contraption Ltd/Parkland Pictures); *A Winter Prince* (Wales Productions); *Caught, Nina Forever* (Jeva Films); *RPG* (MGN Filmes); *Holy Water* (Feature Productions); *Ghost Town* (Haunted Productions).

TV credits include: *Midsomer Murders* (ITV); *Out Of Her Mind* (Stolen Picture); *Treadstone* (Not-4-Not Productions); *The A List* (Kindle Entertainment); *Outlaws, Doctor Foster, Father Brown, New Tricks, Waking The Dead* (BBC); *Shameless* (Channel 4).

Theatre credits include: *Wildefire* (Hampstead Theatre); *Translations* (Sheffield Theatres); *Our Boys* (Duchess Theatre); *The Member Of The Wedding* (Young Vic).

Cian has a great presence in the video-gaming scene, best known as Zane in *Borderlands*.

## André Squire | Husband, Jake, Big John, Doctor

André Squire trained at ITV Workshop, Nottingham; Identity Drama School

Theatre credits include: *One Night in Miami* (ABKCO Theater/ Nottingham Playhouse); *The Grapes of Wrath* (Nuffield

Theatre); *Refugee Boy, Lonely Cowboy* (Leeds Playhouse); *Blue* (Nottingham Arts Theatre); *Measure for Measure, Romeo and Juliet* (ITV Workshop); *Our Style Is Legendary* (Nottingham Playhouse).

Television credits include: *Gormint, Blade Runner 2099* (Amazon Prime); *Suspect: The Shooting of Jean Charles De Menezes* (Etta Pictures); *3 Little Birds* (Tiger Aspect); *FBI International* (CBS Studios); *Nova Jones* (JAM Media); *Worzel Gummidge* (Leopard Pictures); *Gold Digger, A Thing Called Love* (BBC); *Jamie Johnson* (CBBC); *Doctors, West 10 LDN* (Kudos); *Off the Hook* (Greenroom Entertainment/BBC); *The Vice* (Carlton TV).

Film credits include: *Greenland: Migration, BYPASS* (Third Films), *One for the Road* (Film Four)

## Jamie-Rose Monk | Midwife, Sarah, Agent, Julie, Health Visitor, Em, and Mum

Jamie-Rose Monk trained at Mountview Academy of Theatre Arts.

Theatre credits include: *Hansel and Gretel; Princess Essex; The Taming of the Shrew* (Shakespeare's Globe), *Christmas, Actually* (The Southbank Centre); *Greatest Days* (National Tour); *The Witch Finder's Sister* (Queen's Theatre Hornchurch); *Talent* (Sheffield Crucible);

*Dick Whittington* (National Theatre); *A Midsummer Night's Dream* (Bridge Theatre); *The Rise and Fall of Little Voice* (Park Theatre); *Yap Yap Yap* (Southbank Centre/Soho Theatre); *Fat – A One Woman Show* (Hackney Showrooms/Gaggle Productions); *The Poisoners' Pact* (Stuff of Dreams Tour); *Monologue Slam Winner's Edition* (Theatre Royal Stratford East/Triforce Promotions).

Television credits include: *My Lady Jane* (Amazon Studios); *Doctors, Gangsta Granny Strikes Again, Holby City* (BBC*); Class Dismissed* (CBBC); *Gameface* (Objective Fiction).

Film credits include: *Holmes & Watson* (Columbia Pictures Corporation).

Comedy credits include: *Buttery Brown Monk* (Leicester Square Theatre); *The Gag Show* (Gaggle Productions).

Radio credits include: *Sketchtopia – Series 1 & 2* (BBC Radio 4), *Athena's Cancel Culture* (BBC Radio 4)

## Creative & Production Team

### Jane Upton | Writer

Jane Upton's plays include *The Price of Home* (Paines Plough & Derby Theatre: Come to Where I Am, S6); *Finding Nana* (Pleasance Edinburgh Festival, dir Katie Posner, New Perspectives); *All the Little Lights* (Fifth Word/UK tour/Arcola Theatre); *Watching the Living* – an adaptation of two short stories by Daphne Du Maurier (New Perspectives/UK tour); *Swimming* (Menagerie Theatre/Hotbed Festival/Soho Theatre/Edinburgh Festival); *Bones* (Fifth Word/Edinburgh Festival/UK tour).

Jane was the recipient of the 2024 Adopt a Playwright Award.

*All the Little Lights* was nominated Best Play for the 2019 OFFIES and for the 2017 Writers' Guild of Great Britain Awards; it was joint winner of the 2016 George Devine Award for Most Promising Playwright. Jane received a bursary from the Peggy Ramsay Foundation and was shortlisted for CBBC New Voices Initiative.

### Sarah Dickenson | Dramaturg

Brought up in North Cornwall, Sarah Dickenson is a writer and dramaturg with over two decades of experience developing new plays nationally and internationally. As dramaturg she is currently working on projects with Paines Plough, Chichester Festival Theatre, New Perspectives, Jennifer Jackson and Tilted. Her previous roles have included: Associate Dramaturg for Paines Plough, Associate Dramaturg for LAMDA. Associate Dramaturg for the RSC, Production Dramaturg for Shakespeare's Globe, Senior Reader at Soho Theatre, Literary Manager for Theatre503, New Writing Associate at The Red Room. She has been dramaturg on performance projects and artist development nationally and internationally for organisations and theatre makers including: Shakespeare North, Theatre Royal Bury St Edmund's, Minack Theatre, Nuffield Theatre Southampton, Theatre Centre, National Theatre, Bristol Old Vic, Theatre Bristol, Old Vic New Voices, Liverpool Everyman, Theatre Royal Bath, Plymouth Theatre Royal, Tamasha, Apples and Snakes, Almeida, Hall for Cornwall, The Fence and Churchill Theatre Bromley.

As playwright: *The Commotion Time* (Exeter Northcott), *From The Horses Mouth* (O-Region), *Come To Where I'm From* (Paines Plough), *North Ealing* (Theatre503/ Rose Bruford), *PowerPlay* (Hampton Court), *Everything's Fine* (co-writer book, Tilted Co).

She is a recipient of 2025 Playwright 73 award from the Peggy Ramsay Foundation with Exeter Northcott and Shakespeare's Globe.

## Angharad Jones | Director

Angharad Jones is Artistic Director/CEO of New Perspectives. Before joining New Perspectives she co-founded and led new writing company Fifth Word for fifteen years.

Directing credits include: *Model Village* by Anita Sullivan (UK tour); *The Swearing Jar* by Kate Hewlett (UK tour); *The Great Almighty Gill* by Daniel Hoffman-Gill (Edinburgh Fringe/UK tour); script in hand reading of *Maryland* by Lucy Kirkwood; *The Fishermen* by Chigozie Obioma, adapted for the stage by Gbolahan Obisesan (UK tour/West End), for New Perspectives. *LAVA* by James Fritz (world premiere Nottingham Playhouse/Soho/UK tour); *All The Little Lights* by Jane Upton (Associate Director, Nottingham Playhouse/UK tour – joint winner of the George Devine Award and nominated for Best New Play at the Writers' Guild Awards); *Bones* by Jane Upton (Edinburgh Fringe/Tristan Bates Theatre/ UK tour); *Painkillers* by Paul Buie (Edinburgh Fringe & UK tour), for Fifth Word.

New Perspectives co-productions include: *We Need New Names* by NoViolet Bulawayo, adapted for the stage by Mufaro Makubika, directed by Monique Touko with Fifth Word, in association with Brixton House and *Make Good – The Post Office Scandal Musical* by Jeanie O'Hare (book) & Jim Fortune *(music & Lyrics,)* directed by Elle While with Pentabus, marking the Golden Anniversary of both companies.

## Sara Perks | Designer

Sara Perks has designed over 300 shows to date, for UK & world tours, regional theatres, immersive & site specific, West End and National Theatre; and for genres including Shakespeare, classic drama, devised work, family shows, new writing, comedy and musicals.

Current productions include: *Mary and the Hyenas* (Pilot Theatre/Hull Truck); *The Gift* (Park Theatre, London).

Current productions include: *Jesus Christ Superstar* (Spring '25 Scenekvelder, Oslo); *The Mind Mangler* (Virgin Voyagers/ UK tour/West End).

More recent productions include: *Flowers For Mrs Harris* (Riverside Studios, Costume Design – Aria Ents and Tiny Giant); *You Bury Me* – The Women's Playwriting Award from Paines Plough (Bristol Old Vic/Edinburgh Lyceum/Orange Tree); *Good Luck, Studio* (Mischief, Mercury Theatre/ Wiltshire Creative); *The Rise and Fall of Little Voice* (UK Tour Aria/GHF); *71, Coltman Street*, Richard Bean's new play for Hull Truck's 50th Anniversary; UK & International tour of *Footloose* and Tim Firth's new musical *Now Is Good* (Chester Storyhouse).

Other work includes *American Idiot*, *Spamalot*, *Footloose* (West End & UK & International tours); *Hello Dolly!, Gypsy, Hot Stuff!* (Curve); *The King and I* (UK tour); *Beauty Queen of Leenane* (Hull Truck); *Brideshead Revisited* (York/ETT UK tour); the all-female *Oranges and Elephants* (Hoxton Hall, London); the all-female *Posh* (Pleasance Theatre London); *The Suffragette Project* (York Theatre Royal); *Brighton Rock* (Pilot UK tour); *Mother Courage* (Red Ladder – site specific with Pauline McLynn). *Spring Storm/ Beyond The Horizon* (National Theatre & Royal & Derngate, Northampton); *The Mold Riots* (Theatr Clwyd); *Betty Blue Eyes, Sweeney Todd, Turn of the Screw* (UK tours); *Journey's End, Saturday Night and Sunday Morning* and the promenade, multidiscipline, site-specific *Depot* (Mercury Theatre, Colchester).

She was Head of Design for *Shakespeare's Rose Theatre*, York and she designed *Macbeth, Midsummer Night's Dream; Twelfth Night* and *Hamlet,* as well as the theatre stage and facade (2018-19, York & Oxford).

She has held Resident Associate Designer positions at both at Mercury Theatre and ETT, and was nominated for Broadway World Award and What's On Stage Award (*American Idiot*); for an Offie (*Oranges and Elephants* and *Flowers For Mrs Harris*). The latter was awarded Best Off West End Production by *WhatsOnStage* '23. She holds an Edinburgh Fringe First; The John Elvery Theatre Design Award, and a Vision Design (Costume) Award from the BBC.

She holds a BA Hons in Drama & Theatre Studies; and trained in Theatre Design at Bristol Old Vic Theatre School.

More information can be found at saraperkstheatredesign.co.uk

### Lily Woodford | Lighting Designer

Lily Woodford is a London-based lighting designer with experience in technical design and production management. Lily studied at Goldsmiths, University of London where their love of all things beautifully strange was solidified. They thrive on creating work that pushes the boundaries of conventional design to build powerful, thought-provoking spaces. They have worked as a lighting designer for productions such as *Julia Masli: ha ha ha ha ha ha ha, Foreverland* (Southwark Playhouse); *CAttS, Body Show* (Frankie Thompson); *Swarm, Jack the Mack, Body Show* (Liv Ello); *Inside Everyone* (Adrian Bliss); *High Steaks* (Eloina); *Stamptown Comedy* (Stamptown, Jack Tucker).

### Bella Kear | Sound Designer

Bella Kear trained at LAMDA. Her work in theatre includes, as Sound Designer: *Summer 1954* (Theatre Royal Bath/UK tour); *Here In America* (Orange Tree Theatre); *The Good John*

Proctor – Offie-nominated, *Boy in Da Korma* (Jermyn Street Theatre); *The Great Murder Mystery* (The Lost Estate); *Invisible*, *Elephant* and *Clutch* (Bush Theatre); *The Night Woman* (The Other Place); *The Animal Kingdom* (Hampstead Theatre).

As Associate or Assistant Sound Designer: *Mnemonic* (National Theatre); *Newsies* (Troubadour Wembley Park Theatre); *Liberation Squares* (Nottingham Playhouse); *Silence* (Donmar Warehouse); *Edith* (The Lowry); *Blue/Orange* (Theatre Royal Bath/UK tour); *Seven Methods of Killing Kylie Jenner* (Riksteatern); *A Place for We* (Park Theatre); and *Sizwe Banzi is Dead* (MAST Mayflower Studios and tour). Other projects include *Mudlarking*, a sound installation at the Bush Theatre.

## Matt Powell | Projection Design

Matt (they/them) is an Offie-nominated video designer, musical theatre creative and queer practitioner.

Recent video design and digital credits include: *Little Shop of Horrors* (Sheffield Crucible); *Cake: The Marie Antoinette Playlist* (The Other Palace); *The Elixir of Love* (English National Opera); *Brace Brace* (Royal Court); *Ghost Ships* (Icon Theatre); *The Real Ones* (Bush Theatre); *Mother of the Revolution* (Leeds Industrial Museum); *New Year* (Birmingham Opera); *Marie Curie – A New Musical* (Charing Cross Theatre); *Laughing Boy* (Jermyn Street Theatre/Theatre Royal Bath); *Sherlock Holmes and the Poison Wood* (The Watermill Theatre) *Exhibitionists* (King's Head Theatre*); I Really Do Think That This Will Change Your Life* (Pleasance Dome, Edinburgh – Stage Awards for Innovation Finalist/Mercury Theatre, Colchester); *Gypsy in Concert* (Manchester Opera House for Hope Mill Theatre); *Rebecca* (Charing Cross Theatre); *Ride* (The Old Globe/ Curve/Southwark Playhouse); *Animal* (Offie-nominated – Hope Mill Theatre/Park Theatre); *Accidental Death of an Anarchist* (Theatre Royal Haymarket/Sheffield Theatres/ Lyric Hammersmith); *Rumi: The Musical* (D'asha Performing Arts Festival and London Coliseum); *Flight* (Royal College of Music).

## Lucy Glassbrook | Movement Director

Lucy Glassbrook is a Movement Director and Intimacy Director from the Midlands. She has a master's degree in Movement Directing and Teaching from Royal Central School of Speech and Drama and has trained and worked professionally as an actor and dancer. She has always loved physical storytelling and explores movement languages to enable embodied storytelling, character creation and devising, through a consent-based inclusive practice. Her theatrical work contributed to an Offie-nomination for Best New Play *Lately* (Profoca Theatre). She also teaches at various institutions around the UK in Movement practices such as Laban, Animal Studies, Somatic Movement and Intimacy workshops.

Theatre includes: *Pontypool* (Wales Millenium Centre); *Little Women* (HOME/Pitlochry Theatre); *Thrown* (National Theatre of Scotland); *Bindweed* (Arcola/Mercury Theatre); *Cyrano De Bergerac*, *Wuthering Heights* (Birmingham REP); *Fighting Irish* (Belgrade Theatre); *Pride and Prejudice* (Curve Theatre); *Flashbang* (Proforca Theatre); *Hansel and Gretel* (Nottingham Playhouse); *SONDER* (Centrality Theatre).

Mass Movement includes: Dance Captain, Opening and Closing ceremonies of the Commonwealth Games 2022 and Assistant Movement Director & Choreographer City of Culture Opening Ceremony.

### Jessy Roberts | Assistant Director

Jessy Roberts is a director and dramaturg who trained at Bristol Old Vic Theatre School and The University of York. She is Senior Reader at the National Theatre, Associate Director of The Rondo Theatre and Bomb Factory Theatre, and a New Associate with New Perspectives. Recent credits as Director include: *The Incredibly Scary Object* (Jack Studio Theatre); *PAKIt In* (R&D, New Perspectives); *Tap Root* (The Glitch); *THIRST* (Vaults Festival); *Untitled Sparkly Vampire Play* (Omnibus Theatre); *Girls With Wings & Trauma* and *BRANDED* (Bomb Factory Theatre).

As Assistant Director: *Octopolis* (Hampstead Theatre); *Everybody Wants To be Ronaldo* (Tectum Theatre/Birmingham Rep); *Broken Lad* (Arcola Theatrer); *Absolute Scenes* (Motion Bristol); *Crimes Camera Action* (Theatre Royal Bath).

## Director's Note

As an Artistic Director, I read a lot of plays – a lot of good plays, a lot of brilliant plays – but it's still rare to come across one that screams as loudly as this play did to me. I think it's because I felt its rage. It was an immortalisation of feelings I'd carried in my body that I didn't have the words for. I always have to ask *Am I the right person to tell this story?* As a woman in the theatre industry outside of London, and as a mother of twins, I didn't have to reach far for the answer. This one felt personal.

The development of the script has been one filled with care and collaboration, thought, graft and rigour. What Jane has created is an exceptional text that is formally playful, intricately crafted, and inherently theatrical. The play doesn't let us rest easy – traversing and blurring imagination and reality, and demanding we confront our own realities and projections. At its core, it considers what it means to be a woman and specifically a mother. It speaks to the complexities of formative experiences and the sheer effort it can take to exist in this very specific space.

I am often drawn to directing plays that have the room to be interpreted with an abstracted feel – so this play is an absolute gift for me as a director. I have intentionally taken a stripped-backed approach to lean into the process of creating, as we watch our protagonist wrestle with building her world in the pursuit of truth and connection.

I am grateful to so many people who have supported our journey, including our co-producing partners Royal & Derngate, Northampton with Jesse Jones at the helm, for believing in the play as much as I did and for acknowledging the necessity of seeing new plays on mid-scale stages; the National Theatre Generate programme for providing resources to workshop the play; Sarah Dickenson for supporting Jane and me with such generosity and the brilliantly skilled team of creatives who have realised this production. It has been a privilege to direct this world premiere of (*the*) *Woman* and I'm in no doubt there will be many iterations to come in many glorious forms.

I hope this play can do for others what it has done for me.


In solidarity, Angharad.


P.S. It's also funny.

# (the) WOMAN

Jane Upton

*For*

*Mum and Dad – thank you for the crazy love and freedom from politeness. I wish we could live it all again.*

*Mark – thank you for the precious space to write and for slowly embracing the mess in my wake.*

*Edi and Ren – I hope you don't read this for a very long time. Also, god I love you.*

We did not yet entirely understand that Mother, as imagined and politicised by the societal system, was a delusion. The world loved the delusion more than it loved the mother.

*Deborah Levy,* Things I Don't Want to Know

Without a child I could dance across the sexism of my era, whereas becoming a mother shoved my face right down into it.

*Miranda July,* All Fours

A woman must have money and a room of her own if she is to write fiction.

*Virginia Woolf,* A Room of One's Own

There is no more somber enemy of good art than the pram in the hall.

*Cyril Connelly,* Enemies of Promise

Still, I hope the demands of motherhood… don't preclude her from writing something more substantial next time.

*Dominic Cavendish,* The Telegraph *review of* Mum *by Morgan Lloyd Malcom*
(I loved this play, btw. J.U.)

## Writer's Note

Back in 2019, when I was drowning in a particularly tough period of motherhood, my brother saw a boy (now man) I went out with at school walking through our hometown; he shouted, 'I saw your sister pushing a buggy up Derby Road. I expected more from her!'

When my brother told me about this, I was both furious and wounded. I was already carrying around a big bank of 'things people think about me since I had kids', but this was the one that sparked a fire. After that, I started making notes on my phone of things that occurred to me as I crawled through this intense period of change: systemic 'secrets' I was let into, double standards I came up against, formative feelings I couldn't pick myself out of and a shifting sense of self.

A couple of years later, with all these notes, I started writing this play. But not before I contacted the high-school ex in question, twenty-five years after we broke up, to see if he'd be interested in a Zoom (it was pandemic times) to chat about how that formative relationship had impacted us both. I told him I was a writer now and that even though we were boyfriend and girlfriend in a past life, I often thought about that relationship and how it partly formed the adult that I am. To my shock and surprise, he agreed. A week later, I put my make-up on, blurred out the messy background and tried to make myself look better than a woman who'd had kids in her hometown – more than a woman he expected more of. He didn't show up. Of course he didn't. I sat there for an hour. Nothing. No message. Ghosted, as they say. So, I imagined a meeting instead. And that was the start of this.

Since then, there've been a lot of people who've read it and encouraged me. At the very start there was Jack McNamara, Hannah Stone, Lizzie Twells, Katie Posner, Angharad Jones,

Frances Stickley, Suz Bell, Rosie Wyatt, Michelle Hall, Micheline Steinberg and Helen MacAuley (just writing their names here doesn't do justice to their impact, but word count). Later, when Angharad and New Perspectives agreed to produce the play and commissioned a new draft, dramaturg Sarah Dickenson came on board. I'd always wanted to work with Sarah, but this was the first time – and I can honestly say it felt like a light had been switched on inside me. Sarah has played a huge part in the creation of this play and I am so inspired by her wisdom. Angharad organised and directed some brilliant research and development and I am so grateful to the NT Studio and all the actors and creatives who helped shape the work including Archie Backhouse, Fanta Barrie, Jessica Clark, Ray Fearon, Akiya Henry, Jennifer Jackson, Jessy Roberts, Sara Perks, Sabrina Sandhu, Jay Taylor, Jason Williamson and Rosie Wyatt.

So that's how (the) Woman came to be. The gestation period, I suppose. A really, really long one. Longer than an elephant's. And here's the baby. Imperfect, like we all are, but full of questions.

It takes a village.

J. U.

**Characters**

*in order of appearance*

M
MIDWIFE
MATT
BIG JOHN
JOSH
JAKE
HUSBAND
SARAH
AGENT
JULIE
HEALTH VISITOR
DAUGHTER
EM
JOE
DOCTOR
MUM
BABY
JONATHAN DARCY

## A Note About Production

In the first production, all the characters except M were played
by three actors multi-roling. We only had one rule for this – that
the actor who played Matt did not also play Husband. But all
of this is up for grabs. Many layers of meaning can be made
and found in different combinations and you have the freedom
to find them. This play could definitely be done with sixteen
actors, it could be done with a cast of women, it's open for
discovery.

I've included scene titles to support the idea that M is writing
the play as she works her way through this intense period of her
life. You're welcome to use the titles in your production, or not.

At the end of the play is a review. This can be performed, lip-synched, given to an audience member to read, printed on a free sheet, or just left unshared in the script.

The song in Scene One was composed using references from various musicals. Feel free to have fun with that. We did.

## Notes on the Text

The absence of full stops at the end of lines of dialogue indicates an unfinshed sentence or thought.

A forward slash (/) at the end of a line indicates that the following line should overlap it.

An extra line space after a line of dialogue indicates a beat, pause or hesitation before the next line.

*This text went to press before the end of rehearsals and so may differ slightly from the play as performed.*

**Scene One**

**A New Beginning (1)/Detonation**

*Calm. Peace. Dim warm lights come up on* M *in bed with a baby. She is perfectly made up, glowing from the inside of her sweet, rosy, motherly flesh and wearing a long, virginal white nightgown (like Maid Marian in the rape scene from* Robin Hood: Prince of Thieves).

*Music starts to play.*

M. Hello. Hi. Hi.

I'm your mummy.

Yes, I am. Yes, I am.

*Music starts. Singing like Julie Andrews.*

Ten perfect fingers

Ten perfect toes

Skin as soft as velvet

Tiny button nose

Here we are

You and me

It makes sense

Now I see

What life is all about

(*To the* DOCTORS/MIDWIVES – *speaking.*) Excuse me!

*They ignore her.*

(*Singing again.*) Up until this moment

My head was all a mess

Drowning in confusion

Things I can't confess

But that's all gone

My life is new

I'll be perfect

Just for you

A brand-new shiny me

(*To the* DOCTORS/MIDWIVES – *louder now*.) Excuse me!

*No one is listening.*

*She climbs out of bed. The bottom of her dress is completely soaked in blood like a nightmare.*

*A beat kicks in.*

*She moves into spoken word – Lin-Manuel Miranda style – perhaps the* MEDICAL STAFF *join in on a set dance piece.*

Baby girl, comrade, sister

I'm gonna raise you up, won't try to fix ya

I'll celebrate your traits and never judge ya

Let you trash boundaries and always love ya

When acne plagues your face I'll kiss your skin

Won't nail-poke your belly

We'll destroy the word slim – (MEDICAL STAFF *join in*.) ICK!

We'll hail high our sisters and roar our truth

Occupy space and smash the roof

This is our moment, we're power manifested

We're the toil our foremothers invested

Obliterate the patriarchy, slam the system

One mess at a time, too many to list them

From here I will be better

From here I'm growing up

From here I've found my voice

From here I'm showing up

*The riff from 'Under Pressure' by Queen and David Bowie plays.*

*She breaks away from the musical number – to* DOCTORS/ MIDWIVES, *who continue to ignore her.*

Excuse me!

*Suddenly the noise of the ward is audible. It is loud. Babies crying. Women giving birth.*

*Beat speeds up.*

*Speaking now, like time is running out. But still the image is messily reminiscent of a Madonna and Child painting.*

And I'll hold you

And I'll tell you you're the best thing that ever existed

I'll fill you so stuffed full of your own brilliance that nothing dark will ever get through the cracks

But I'll make you aware of your own privilege

And I'll show you the world isn't fair

And that there are very bad people

But

Also

We'll have so much fun

And I'll make sure you're never sad, or lost, or lonely, and that you never give your body to anyone who doesn't deserve it

No matter how beautiful they are. Or good at playing guitar.

Everything you need, I'll give to you

Perfectly

To ensure you are top-to-toe full

Of electric confidence.

A strong independent woman

Who never doubts her own worth

NEVER

(*To* MIDWIFE.) What's happening? Excuse me!

MIDWIFE *comes but is very busy and distracted.*

She's not crawling up to the areola like they said she would.

MIDWIFE (*starts handling the baby and the breast roughly, pushing the baby on to M's nipple*). Right. Let me just

M. I've read all the books. I know how to do it. She's just not

MIDWIFE. You've got to squeeze your nipples. Really hard.

M. Oh, OW, excuse me, that's my, OWWWWW

MIDWIFE. You've got to force the milk down. Keep squeezing.

M (*fighting back tears, basically violated*). Ow. Owwwwww!

MIDWIFE. Oh come on!

M. I've got another contraction

MIDWIFE. Have you delivered the placenta?

M. What?

MIDWIFE. That's it. Push. Push

M. Push? Owwwww.

*Placenta drops out on an umbilical cord.*

I never saw this in the movies! Or the nativity

MIDWIFE. Men wrote that, love.

*The* MIDWIFE *cuts the cord and goes to take the placenta away.*

Hang on, don't I want to fry that or bake it or something?

Right.

*The* MIDWIFE *dumps the placenta in a large plastic bucket.*

M. She's still not

MIDWIFE *squeezes her boob again.*

MIDWIFE. You've got to squeeze – (*To another mother.*) I'm coming!

M. Ow, please don't

MIDWIFE. You have to keep (*to another mother, opposite side to the last.*) I'm coming!

MIDWIFE *leaves. Baby is screaming.*

*Music swells up again into climax.*

M *sings like Julie Andrews.*

This is a new day, a fresh start, a second chance, for me

A brand-new start for me.

M *checks no one is looking and rearranges the placenta next to her. She pulls her selfie stick out and takes the perfect picture, hiding all the chaos and detritus.*

*She drops everything including the baby. Loads of bottles fall from the sky.*

## Scene Two

## Top of the Pops/Self Harm

M *has gone to find her high-school boyfriend* MATT *on a crappy market stall in the town.*

MATT'*s mate* BIG JOHN *is running another stall close by and stands in earshot.*

MATT. Alright.

M. Hi.

MATT *recognises* M.

MATT. Jesus.

M. Yeah.

MATT (*about the buggy*). That yours then?

M. Yep.

MATT. God, how long's it been?

M. Twenty years.

MATT. Must be. The years have not been kind, eh?

M. Likewise. Got any of these towels in white?

MATT. That is white.

M. Looks like dried spunk. I'll leave it.

MATT. Suit yourself.
     Jesus. Can't believe

M. What?

MATT. When I saw you with the buggy.

M. What?

MATT. No, I just, expected

M. What?

MATT. More

M. More than what?

MATT. Kids. You. Here.

M. You still live here.

MATT. Yeah, but

M. You expected me to do more with my life than have kids in *our* hometown?

MATT. Yeah.

M. Like what?

MATT. I dunno.

M. No, come on

MATT. No. I mean. *Top of the Pops*.

M. *Top of the Pops*?

MATT. You were always good at singing.

M. And you thought

MATT. I just thought one day I'd be sitting in my armchair with a beer flicking through the channels and suddenly you'd be there in some sequinned-bikini thing, loads of mad make-up, dancing like some crazy fucking fire woman and I'd just start

M. What?

MATT. Wanking, I suppose.

M. Right.

What is it about this then that disgusts you?

MATT. I didn't say disgust

M. That's not enough for you?

MATT. Don't be like that.

M. Like what?

MATT. Is that a crime? To think that? Of everyone at school I just didn't see you

M. What?

MATT. Doing this. It's a fucking compliment.

M. So who did you see doing this?

MATT. I dunno. Marie Marshall. Natalie Smith. That sort. Look, I just thought, when we went out

M. Fucked on that field

MATT. A few times

M. Fucked on that field a few times

MATT. We went for a beer

M. Did we?

MATT. In The Bell.

M. We got thrown out.

MATT. We went to the offie a lot. Anyway, I just

M. What? You thought, she's going to change things, as I laid back on that dog-shit-stained grass and let you cum over my eyelids

MATT. Okay, yeah

M. Cool

MATT. You were, I dunno, different

M. Different?

MATT. From the other girls. That's why I went out with you

M. Fucked in a field

MATT. That's another compliment. You need to learn to take compliments.

M. No. Honestly. Thank you.

MATT. You were always so free. So up for it.

M. Up for what?

MATT. A laugh. Anything, really. You were fucking cool. Not tight like most of them. And clever, as well, straight-A student. An unusual combination in a girl. Look, I don't wanna have a fucking debate about it.

M. Course not

MATT. I don't wanna justify my words. I'm just saying. What?

M. I want to know what it is about this that bothers you.

MATT. Alright then.

M. Go on.

MATT. The smell.

M. You can smell me from there?

MATT. I can imagine. The smell.

M. Right.
    Does your mum smell?

MATT. Don't be fucking tight.

M. Genuine question.

MATT. Well, I don't have to consider fucking her, do I, so my
    nose is not attuned to that.

M. What else?

MATT. Your cunt's probably been split in two. Deformed.
    Because you're a bit older. It won't've healed properly.
    A proper axe wound, you might say.

M. Nice.

MATT. I imagine it and it

M. What?

MATT. Kind of makes me sick.

M. Right.

MATT. And you probably piss yourself when you laugh, so
    if I was laughing with you I'd start to smell piss. And that
    would upset me, I suppose. It would ruin the joke. It wasn't
    meant to be like that.

M. No.

MATT. I wanted you to stay like you were on that field.
    I wanted you to preserve yourself and then do something
    amazing. And I could say 'I fucked her. I came over her

eyelids' when you were there, fit as fuck on *Top of the Pops*.
I could turn to my wife and kids and tell them that.

M. Yeah, I can understand that.

MATT. But this. This is just embarrassing. You've got a hole
in your leggings. And your face is sort of red raw. Like an
alcoholic old man. If my kids saw you, I wouldn't tell them.

M. Right.

So would you now?

MATT. What?

M. Fuck me?

MATT. Course.
I wouldn't be proud of it though.

M. No.

MATT. Just being honest. Best policy.

M. I didn't expect you to do anything. By the way.

MATT. Stuck-up bitch.

M. I expected you to be selling stolen towels on a shit stall on
a shitty street where you're not allowed to be.

MATT. Basic fucking /

M. Just my opinion. Just being honest.

MATT. You'd better shut your fucking mouth.
Do you want any towels or what? Tenner to you. Mate's
rates.

M. You're alright.

*She goes to leave. Stops. Exhales with every fucking inch of
her body.*

Fuck's sake.

MATT. What?

M. Do you remember that house party?

MATT. Which one?

M. At Matt Shaw's? We went to his little brother's bedroom.

MATT. Yeah.

M. I think about that a lot.

MATT. Still?

M. Yeah. I mean, I hate you, I think you're the world's biggest prick.

MATT. GOT the world's biggest prick.

M. I actually came here to kill you. Metaphorically. But yeah, Matt Shaw's brother's bedroom. I wank over that. God, I might even wank over this.

MATT. Today?

M. Yeah.

MATT. Why?

M. Because I'm wrung out the wrong way round, to be honest with you.

MATT. You're all over the place.

M. I am.

MATT. You wanna pull yourself together.

M. I do.

MATT. You're not meant to wank over a dickhead like me. It's

M. Regressive.

MATT. Yeah.

M. Sordid. Pathetic. Misogynistic.

MATT. Yeah. And that.
You're lucky. You can do anything now. This is your time. Taking over.

M. That's what they say.

MATT. Who?

M. People like you.

MATT. We're history. But you. You can write whatever you like. That's why…

M. …this is disappointing.

MATT. So many people are going to be disappointed.

M. Thanks for the feedback.

MATT. Any time. It's bolstered me, if I'm honest.

Don't suppose

M. What?

MATT. Want a fuck. In my van?

M. It doesn't mean I think you're a good person.

MATT. Course not.

M. Don't tell women about this.

MATT. What women?

M. All women. Essentially this is offensive.
Or men. Don't tell men.
Don't tell my mum and dad.
Or my husband.
Or my daughter. She wouldn't understand.

MATT. No worries. John, can you watch the kid, mate?

John's a legend. He's got twelve.

M. Great.

MATT. This is really sad by the way.

M. It is. I'm not the sort of woman who should be allowed in a play. And your van is disgusting.

MATT. I've fucked about fifty in there.

M. Stop with the foreplay. I don't want to be turned on.

MATT. Why not?

M. I'm clinging to the hope that in some small way I've evolved.

MATT. Right?

M. Let's just get on with it.

*They have sex.*

Fuck it, that was actually good.

MATT. You did well. You wanna towel for your face?

*He chucks her what he thinks is a towel but it's a Babygro.*

Oh, hang on I've got a load of knock-off Babygros if you want one for the kid?

M. You're alright

MATT. What is it again? Girl?

I've got

'Not all girls are princesses – some are superheroes!'

'Riots not diets'

'Hashtag you go girl'

'Retired hot girl'

'Too busy changing the world'

M. Where's my daughter?

MATT. John, where's the kid?

BIG JOHN. Shit, I sold her with a couple of bed sheets.

M. I knew I'd lose her if I had filthy sex in a van.

Which way did they go?

*BIG JOHN looks around.*

BIG JOHN. Erm

M. HELP!

MATT. 'A girl should be two things – who and what she wants'

M. HELP!

MATT. 'Who runs the world? Girls!'

M. HELP!

### Scene Three

### The Commission/Contortion

*Inside an office in a big London theatre – walls dripping with cultural capital.*

JOSH. So, we absolutely loved *Riot*.

M. Thank you.

JOSH. Deeply affecting, deeply moving.

JAKE. Shocking. In many ways.

JOSH. And tight, so tight, structurally.

JAKE. We loved it.

JOSH. Honestly. Congratulations.

JAKE. And on the awards.

JOSH. We noticed it before the awards, it's just we've been absolutely

JAKE. Stacked.

JOSH. Stacked, exactly

M. Of course! Thank you.

JOSH. It's a huge step up for you, from your previous stuff. Do you feel that?

M. I suppose so.

JAKE. A huge step up.

JOSH. So we just wanted to get you in really to talk about any ideas you've got for your next piece. We would absolutely love to work with you.

M. Wow.

JOSH. We do have a pot for new commissions and we'd be fascinated to hear your thoughts.

M. That's amazing, thank you.

JOSH. Nope. No need to say thank you. This is something we talk about a lot here.

M. Sorry.

JAKE. Oops, no sorrys either.

JOSH. Sorry is banned in this office. Just, tell us what's next for you. What do you want to write?

M. Okay. So. I'm not great at pitching.

JOSH. Don't apologise before you've begun. This is just a chat.

JAKE. Simple.

JOSH. Go for it.

M. It's maybe a bit

JOSH. No. Seriously. You're brilliant. Go for it!

M. Okay.
I want to write a play about motherhood.

But obviously not, boring, not the boring stuff, it's about how, well,
it's really hard to explain, sorry, I haven't really figured it /

JOSH. Go on.

JAKE. No pressure.

M. Okay, it's about, I think, all these different, conflicting feelings of, how you pass over this invisible threshold, that you didn't, necessarily, how, I guess like all the things that formed you, as a woman, as a teenager, the way society makes you

Erm

Okay. I have this idea for one scene where she's just had a baby and she's in this, a state of disorientation I suppose, and she goes back to see her ex-boyfriend from school, so she can, erm, do you know what I'm sort of

JAKE. Erm

JOSH. So, let me get this, you want to write about the female experience of parenthood? I mean, what even is the female experience? Can we even categorise it these days?

M. No, I know. It's complicated. It's not really about a homogenised female experience. It's very personal, guts on a page

JAKE. Autobiographical?

M. Not exactly.

JAKE. Okay

JOSH. Good. No, this is good. Do you mind if Jake and I just talk a bit about what we've been discussing?

M. Oh God, of course. Absolutely.

JOSH. Okay. Hear me out for a second. Obviously, taking into account everything you've just said. Have you thought about a thriller?

M. Erm

JOSH. A really tightly crafted thriller.

JAKE. Preferably with police.

JOSH. Obviously in a way only you could write.

M. Okay

JOSH. A thriller about motherhood, if you like. Maybe this woman, has this baby but it starts to see things. Or predict the future. And no one believes her.

M. But what? It's post-natal depression, maybe? She's imagining it?

JOSH. Possibly. Or, the baby is actually seeing things. Maybe the ghosts of unsolved crimes.

M. Okay.

JAKE. Or, how about she's a pregnant police detective who gets involved in something really sinister but all the way through the pregnancy is completely unmentioned, like not even acknowledged.

JOSH. That's interesting.

M. Right. Yeah. Okay. Sorry. Oh God, no, not sorry, I mean. I think I just wanted to tell a story that a lot of women will relate to. Just a kind of raw

JAKE. Raw, okay

JOSH. Raw. Yep. Or. Have you ever thought about a musical?

M. Erm

JOSH. Gone are the days when raw and musical were mutually exclusive terms! On a real, layperson level, think less

JAKE. Andrew Lloyd Webber, yeah?

JOSH. Exactly. Exactly. More

JOSH *and* JAKE. Lin-Manuel!

M. Maybe, I could, include songs.

JOSH. Maybe? But, what? Be honest.

Look, what you're describing, from experience, there's not really an audience for that. The people that have gone through that, they're not buying theatre tickets.

M. Why not?

JOSH. They're usually pinned under a baby somewhere.

Seriously. On a bigger note. We don't really want to show women having babies.

M. Why not?

JOSH. Because they're capable of so much more. If we keep
showing women pregnant, dying, ill, being murdered, raped
et cetera

JAKE. It's just not redressing the balance.

JOSH. Exactly. Look, we've got you here because we know you
can deliver us strong, feisty, sassy

JAKE. Kick-ass

JOSH. Kick-ass, exactly, kick-ass twenty-first century women.
Fine, if they've got kids, fine, but it's like they haven't
dictated their life, y'know?

M. Right.

JOSH. Look at you. You've got a kid, right?

M. Yeah.

JOSH. But you're here, pitching /

JAKE. Chatting /

JOSH. Chatting to us. I mean, where's your kid?

M. She's outside.

JAKE. It's snowing.

M. Yeah, my mum's walking her round in the buggy. It's the
only way she'll sleep.

JOSH. You've got your mum helping you, which is fantastic.
Are you staying in town?

M. Oh, erm, no, we got the fast train down this morning

JOSH. Fast train, great, so everything's pretty accessible then,
to pop in and out?

M. Yeah, I mean, it did cost two-hundred and fifty pounds.

JOSH. You're investing in an exciting future though.

M. Definitely. What exactly is the commission?

JOSH. Yep. Good question. It's a seed commission.

JAKE. Fifteen hundred pounds.

JOSH. But against a full commission if we like the first draft.

M. First full draft? A whole play?

JOSH. Well, yes.

M. I'm not sure that'll stretch to childcare. I've got a mortgage and

JOSH. This is a crucial point in your career

M. No, of course, I know.

JOSH. Great. So. What do you think? Do you want to have another go at pitching to us?

M. Erm, I might need a bit of

JOSH. Come on. Take the chance.

M. Alright. Erm. Okay.

I want to write a play that is definitely not a one-woman show about the minutiae of motherhood. It's not a woman whining on about milk leaks or vaginal tears or losing her identity. That's not entertainment. It's not a man-bashing, feminist

JAKE. We love feminist

M. It is feminist, but not an oversimplified look at gender roles and sexual politics.

Oh. Yes! And there's a baby that sees ghosts. And crimes. It can solve crimes before they actually happen. But it's a baby. So the police don't take it too seriously at first. Until it, busts something up. Something big. Drugs and rapes and murders and ghosts.

But there are no women getting raped. By the way. And all the murder victims are men. But the baby is a girl.

And there might be songs.

JOSH *and* JAKE. Fantastic.

**Scene Four**

**Ultimatum/Twisted Climax**

M *and her* HUSBAND *have just had sex.*

HUSBAND. I hate that.

M. What?

HUSBAND. Sex like that.

M. Like what?

HUSBAND. It felt like you didn't want it.

M. I didn't.

HUSBAND. So why did you then?

M. Because you wanted it.

HUSBAND. I only want it if you want it.

M. That's not true.

HUSBAND. I don't want to fuck a corpse.

M. You get angry if we don't have sex for a week.

HUSBAND. I don't get angry.

M. Moody then.

HUSBAND. I can't help it if I want to have sex with you.

M. I can't help it if I don't want to have sex with you.

HUSBAND. Am I that unattractive?

M. It's not even about that.

HUSBAND. What is it about then?

M. I'm totally knackered.

HUSBAND. So sex will relax you.

M. Sleep will do that just fine.

HUSBAND. You sleep so much.

M. Are you kidding? I haven't slept for two years.

HUSBAND. Neither have I.

M. I'm tired.

HUSBAND. Of me?

M. Of the world.

HUSBAND. So why go through with it?

M. Because you're all over me and you won't stop until it's done.

HUSBAND. You make me sound like a

M *shrugs as if to confirm.*

What the fuck is that?

M. I'm just saying, I would know if you didn't want to have sex and I would stop.

HUSBAND. So say stop.

M. I shouldn't have to.

HUSBAND. But you could.

M. I could.

HUSBAND. So why don't you?

M. It's easier to get it over with.

HUSBAND. What have I done wrong now?

M. Nothing. I'm sick of explaining myself.

My darling, it's not that I don't love your quirky burrowing penis, it's just that a tornado of hormones has torn through my body like locusts, taken part of my life, my brain, my libido, changed me as a person, and I am knackered ALL THE TIME. But little Willy Wonka is still utterly adorable to me /

HUSBAND. / Oh fuck off

M. / and has done NOTHING wrong and while I sleep here you may place him in my mouth whenever you like. Okay?

HUSBAND. I wouldn't mind but when we met you were all over me.

M. Yeah, and you kept me at arm's length.

HUSBAND. It was a bit off-putting. I couldn't work out what was wrong with you.

M. Because I was sexually confident?

HUSBAND. Aggressive.

M. I wanted you. Which is such a weird thing to say fifteen years later, here, dressed like this, with all we know now.

HUSBAND. You don't want me any more?

M. I do. I want you so much. I want you to stroke me like a cat and rub my boobs without getting turned on in the slightest, while I drink hot chocolate. I don't want anyone else to do that except you.

HUSBAND. I feel like you got me here under false pretences.

M. So you married me because you thought I'd always be up for it?

HUSBAND. No. But you were so different back then.

M. What can I say? I like sex with people I don't know. I like making them like me by giving good sex.

HUSBAND. And what about when you do know them?

M. It's awkward.

HUSBAND. Awkward with people you know, people you're married to, but not with people you don't?

M. I can't grind in fantasy underwear because you know what my cunt looks like. I don't want to flick my eyes at you while sucking your cock after I saw you silently scoffing that

six-pack of doughnuts last night on the baby monitor. You sat
with me while I did my first shit after I was torn apart by the
baby. How can I have good, slamming sex while all of that is
swilling around my brain? I would be embarrassed to try and
be sexy.

HUSBAND. You are sexy.

M. Seriously.

HUSBAND. Seriously.

M. Not sexy enough to turn me on though. To turn me on,
I need to be a fantasy like they said I should be. I can't be
your fantasy because you know too much. And I know you
know too much. My joints ache and I've got piles, again,
and I haven't shaved anywhere. In months. I'm basically
disgusting.

HUSBAND. I don't care.

M. Why would I want to fuck when I feel gross? When you
look gross, no offence, and stink of onions and stale coffee?
When I'm angry and bored and wrung out. Why would I?

HUSBAND. For me.

M. So I have to heave myself out of slumber so you can dump
your load and sleep better?
Anyway

HUSBAND. What?

M. I searched your porn history. You said you'd stopped
watching it.

HUSBAND. What do you expect?

M. I expect you to stop watching it.

HUSBAND. So you don't want sex and you don't want me
watching other people have sex.

M. You watched 'stepdaughter fucks her stepdad'.

HUSBAND. I just click on the one that looks good in the brief
five-minute window I get on my own.

M. And the one that looked good was 'stepdaughter fucks her stepdad'?

HUSBAND. You were dressed as a St Trinian when we met.

M. It was a fancy-dress party. Fifteen years ago. And we didn't have a daughter.

HUSBAND. It's a fantasy, isn't it? Age old. Not actual schoolgirls. But that look.

M. If that's the fantasy, how can I ever trust you with my middle-aged body?

HUSBAND. You know what I mean. You were dressed as a St Trinian and on the pull.

M. I've evolved

HUSBAND. Have you?

M. I unpicked it and I've evolved. And it's fucked up.

HUSBAND. I've seen your porn history too. You haven't evolved very far.

M. Why are you searching my history?

HUSBAND. Why are you searching mine?

M. And what about when our daughter has sleepovers and brings her teenage friends here. What am I meant to do then? Assume you aren't attracted to them?

HUSBAND. Fuck off.

M. Well, it's the same thing.

HUSBAND. It's not the same thing.

*Glitch.*

I have layers of my brain. My brain is complex.

M. Is that true, really?

*Glitch.*

HUSBAND. I have layers of my brain. My brain is complex.

M. I'm not sure. I mean, you watch that shit, it bleeds in, right. You can't help that.

*Glitch.*

HUSBAND. I have layers of my brain. My brain is complex. You have to just silently accept that or lose your shit completely.

M. Right.

HUSBAND. What do you actually want?

M. Connection. Intimacy I suppose. A laugh.

HUSBAND. But not sex?

M. My brain won't switch off and allow it. I'm sorry. It might change.

HUSBAND. When, though? When do you think you might want sex again?

M. I mean I do want sex.

HUSBAND. What?

M. Yeah. With people I don't know. Preferably an old man with dirty hands.

HUSBAND. Great. Well, I'm pretty old and I could rub my hands around the bathroom.

M. Is that a dig about the state of the bathroom?

HUSBAND. No.

M. You can clean the bathroom.

HUSBAND. I'm pretty busy, day to day.

M. And I'm not?

HUSBAND. You have more time in the house than me.

M. Yeah, and I'm looking after our daughter.

HUSBAND. I know.

M. And I'm good at it.

HUSBAND. Yeah.

M. We do loads. And it's hard work.

HUSBAND. I know.
But she goes to nursery two days.

M. And on nursery days I am trying to work.

HUSBAND. What are you working on?

M. Don't start this.

HUSBAND. I'm interested. Honestly.

M. I'm trying to write the play. The same play.

HUSBAND. When do you think they'll give you the full
contract?

M. I told you, I've got to finish a draft.

HUSBAND. Well what's the plan for that? Genuinely.

M. Let's not go into this now, please.
I am here, day in day out, looking after our kid.

HUSBAND. You have two full days

M. And basically I spend them trying to remember who the fuck
I am.

HUSBAND. Believe me, I would love to spend two days
finding myself while you pay the mortgage.

M. Right, and you think this conversation will convince me to
shag you, how exactly? Are you hoping I might provide sex
in lieu of salary?

HUSBAND. We promised ourselves we would never be these
people. When we met, we both said we would never be these
people.

M. We were clueless, cocky pricks and we didn't have a toddler.

HUSBAND. We sit and watch TV every night.

M. We are boring, disappointing, domestic clichés.

HUSBAND. I didn't want to be.

M. You think I did?

HUSBAND. I can't live like this indefinitely.

*Glitch.*

M. So that's an ultimatum, is it? Fuck me or I'm off?

HUSBAND. Yep.

*Glitch.*

M. So that's an ultimatum, is it? Fuck me or I'm off.

HUSBAND. Of course not. But if you're telling me I have to live a life without mutually fulfilling sex, then I have to think really carefully about how I would cope with that. If I could cope with that.

*Glitch.*

M. Right. So that's an ultimatum, is it? Fuck me or I'm off.

HUSBAND. Yeah. Let me give you a UTI while I ram your own day-full-of-dirt inside you. Let me fuck you in this heightened state of anger so you get a blinding headache and can't sleep while you listen to me snore having sprayed my seed all over your disgusting overgrown bush.


I love you.

M. Yeah.

HUSBAND. I really, really do.

M. I know.

## Scene Five

## Very Mindful.../Fucking Her Up

M *is on a day trip with her daughter.*

M. Ahhh, isn't this amazing? The sunshine and the water and, oh look at the lambs, there look, so sweet, look, darling, there, the little lambs, aren't we lucky? Wow, it's so pretty.

Let's get a picture. (*She gets her phone out and starts scrolling.*) Picture for Daddy, to show him what we're up to. Oh, wow. Fuck. Fuck. Will you look at that. Layla Jones got a BAFTA. Layla Jones is a very young woman Mummy worked with once. Wow. Well done, Layla. That. Is. Brilliant. She. Is. Brilliant.

Right. Let's get a photograph. That's right. Okay, look here. Here. Smile. Smile, darling. Look at the camera and smile. Properly. Stop squinting your eyes. Open them, now. Right, smile or we're going home. We're going home unless you look at the camera and smile. Now. No ice cream then, that's it, okay, no ice cream. Thank you.

## Scene Six

## Big Night Out/Busted

M *is at the pub with her old mate* SARAH.

SARAH. I'm getting the double bacon burger.

M. I thought you were vegan now?

SARAH. Only on Mondays.
    In January.
    Ve-gan-u-ary.
    And
    extra fries.
    Fuck off!

M. I didn't say anything!

SARAH. I'm doing this stupid fasting thing where I eat nothing for like sixteen hours a day so these are my banqueting hours, baby. I did my ten thousand steps as well, as monitored by my spy watch. So. I deserve it, thank you. What are you getting?

M. I'm not that hungry.

SARAH. Still skint?

M. No. Bit. But

SARAH. I'll sub you. Sold a load of fake perfume this week. I can get you on the scheme.

M. You're alright.

SARAH. You make money, I make money, amigo.

M. Nah, it's fine, I've got a job, I am actually not that hungry.

SARAH. Can I just say, I cannot believe we are sitting here on our own with a bottle of wine! For the first time in, what?

M. Nearly three years.

SARAH. Must be. We gonna go into town?

M. Yeah?

SARAH. CELEBRATE GOOD TIMES, COME ON!

M. Nutter.

SARAH. Nice to feel a bit like ourselves though, innit?

M. Yeah.
    So what else is going on?

SARAH. Yeah, right, actual news. Oh God.

M. What?

SARAH. I went to Charlie's hen do in Liverpool. So funny.

M. Why wasn't I invited?

SARAH. You wouldn't be into that. Very low cultural bar. We
went to The Cavern in dick hats, it was hilarious. We went
shopping on the Sunday and Charlie had to puke into a vase
in M&S.

M. You're kidding?

SARAH. Nightmare. What else? Oh God, it was Wendy's
funeral, as you know. So that was awful. And the kids
refused to wear black. Little'n went in a yellow-spandex
dance outfit, so Wendy would've disapproved of that no
doubt. Which pissed me off. I was pissed off at my mother-
in-law at her own funeral.

M. Ah, mate, that sounds complicated.

SARAH. She had 'We'll Meet Again' as her send-off song. I
fucking hope not.

M. How's Lee coping with it?

SARAH. He just wants loads of sex. But he's sad all the time,
so I sort of have to dip into my – (*Tapping her brain.*) go-to
cum library, you know what I mean?

M. Have you still got one?

SARAH. I mean it's glitchy. I swear that's why people have
affairs, just to top it up.

M. But you don't mind?

SARAH. What?

M. Having excessive sex with a sad man that you see every
day?

SARAH. It's not ideal. I mean, I literally married him because
he could turn his steering wheel with the palm of his hand,
if I break it down. He used to excrete testosterone. So, yeah,
this is a departure. Anyway, what you been up to?

M. Ahh, just kids' stuff, mainly.

SARAH. Aw, what's she up to?

M. Potty training. So everywhere smells like piss.

SARAH. Standard.

M. And, I've been trying to write a play.

SARAH. Ah cool, what's it about?

M. It's the same one, so

SARAH. Remind me

M. Sort of about disentangling from the patriarchy and how
hard that is. I don't really know. I'm really bad at pitching.
I'm cringing just trying to explain it.

SARAH. Oh God, I'm so bad at putting things into words.

M. It's awful, isn't it!

SARAH. My brain just doesn't work when I need it to.

M. Such a relief to say that without anyone telling me not to do
myself down or whatever.

SARAH. So what's it about again? Test it on me.

M. Okay, it's kind of how we, well I, have this need to feel
attractive to men, alongside having all these cerebral
thoughts about what we should be – that we should be more
than that, more than mothers, more than sexual beings, I
don't know, God I'm so crap

SARAH. That sounds heavy. And a bit dull. No offence.

M. Yeah. Well, theatre's not really for you.

SARAH. So, who is theatre for? I never really understand.

M. It's for people who go to the theatre.

SARAH. I saw *Tina Turner the Musical* last year in London,
thank you!

M. No, yeah, I know. It's kind of for people who go a lot.
People who are already thinking along the lines of what
you're writing and you sort of have to bring their thoughts to
them.

SARAH. Right. So theatre is for people who already go to the theatre?

M. Yeah. Because they're the people who buy the tickets. I'm not going to get you to go to the theatre, am I?

SARAH. Not for a disentangling patriarchy type thing.

I've already got my dodgy Fire Stick, apologies, that's all the entertainment I can manage.

M. No, God, totally, I understand that. I mean theatre can be an exhilarating live and communal experience that could change your life.

SARAH. I believe you. You'll smash it anyway.

M. Cheers, mate

SARAH. Wait a minute, am I in it? The play.

M. Right now?

SARAH. Yeah.

M. Yeah, I think so.

SARAH. Wow, so, like, what am I?

M. You're Sarah.

SARAH. Yeah but, what am I, in the play?

M. I guess you're all my actual friends. The ones I don't actually have anything in common with and who wouldn't come to watch my plays, but who've known me forever and would come to the hospital with a bag of my favourite things if I was really sick or something.

SARAH. Wow. Okay. Big responsibility. Sarah be reppin'. Who else is in it?

M. Matt from school.

SARAH. Fucking-on-Ransom-Field Matt?

M. Yeah.

SARAH. Jesus, wept? Why you putting that prick in it? Are you ever going to get over that?

M. Probably not.

SARAH. Well, sounds decent. I might come and see this one. If I'm in it, like.

M. Obviously.

SARAH. You alright? You've gone dead pale.

M. I feel a bit... it's that fried-food smell

SARAH. You've not touched your wine.

M. I have

*She takes a big gulp but struggles swallowing it.*

SARAH. You're pregnant, aren't you?

M. What? No.

SARAH. I'm a witch with this stuff. Seriously. I knew it soon as you walked in.

M. I'm not pregnant.

SARAH. Lee says I've got some sixth-sense shit for women's stuff.

M. I'm not pregnant, Sarah.

Fuck. I'm pregnant, aren't I?

SARAH. Yep. Shit. Shit.

Ahhhh, babe! Congratulations!

*The other cast members chime in on this barrage of clichés as M starts to fall into oblivion.*

CAST. Now's as good a time as any.

Another chance to get it right.

Keep each other company.

One of each, if you're lucky.

SARAH. Although they say two is easier than one and
I honestly have no idea which crackhead invented that
saying.

CAST. Oh my God, it might be twins.

You've got this!

SARAH. Does that mean we're not going into town?

**Scene Seven**

**The Secret/How To Lie**

M *is in a meeting with her* AGENT.

AGENT. It's so good to see you, darling.

M. You too

AGENT. I've been meaning to call but everything's been crazy.
How are you? How's...

M. She's fine. Great.

AGENT. Good. You look a bit tired.

M. I'm fine. Have you had chance to look at the scenes I sent?

AGENT. I have. Have you written much more, or?

M. Not yet.

AGENT. Right.

M. What did you think?

AGENT. I mean, I can see what you're trying to do.

M. Yeah?

AGENT. Of course.

M. And...

AGENT. And. Is it really urgent enough?

M. Urgent is a big word. I mean, I think so.

I don't see it, the truth of it, anywhere. One minute popular culture was telling us to starve ourselves while dropping to the floor to deliver the perfect blow job, the next it's telling us to raise strong girls, considerate boys, all while weight-training ourselves to body positivity and somehow having fulfilling sex with a person we met in a past life. I feel like I'm going to implode or explode or something.

AGENT. Well, don't do that.

Look, I've had some feedback. There's a slight worry, if you like, that you'll struggle to deliver something beyond a messy, autobiographical… splurge, at this point.

M. Oh. Right. Great.

AGENT. Can I let you into a secret?

M. Okay.

AGENT. This goes no further.

M. Of course.

AGENT. I have a child. Children. I mean, they're practically adults now.

M. Wow. I didn't know that.

AGENT. Don't take it personally. I have members of my own family who don't know. I just don't want that to be part of what they see here. It doesn't serve me. And you have to decide now, as you stick your flag in this tiny patch of sand, whether it's really the way you want them to see *you*. It's a choice. But as soon as it's out there you're no longer a theoretical virgin with endless potential.

M. But surely we're beyond that?

AGENT. Oh, of course we are. No, we are. People say we are. But it takes our collective subconscious years to catch up. We'll be long dead before those ingrained opinions are exorcised, if indeed they ever are. So, in the meantime, you somehow have to squeeze yourself into the system while making it look like you've beaten it.

M. In our initial meeting, after *Love Songs*

AGENT. *Love Songs* was wonderful

M. You said you loved the way my writing offers an unapologetic, raw, gutsy insight into being a modern woman.

AGENT. Absolutely.

M. But that's what this play is.

AGENT. There are aspects of womanhood that are interesting – even to men – young women navigating sex, let's say. But motherhood? I don't think so. In *Riot* you proved that you've got a vital political voice. Some people actually thought it was written by a man, love.

I understand. I do. But, maybe, motherhood as *the* theme is banal.

M. Not to those going through it.

AGENT. I'm sorry. Look, write a journal if that'll help get it out of your system. Your little one's two now?

M. Three. Just

AGENT. The baby years are far behind you. It gets better.

I get it. I do.

My eldest is epileptic. Had his first fit at two years old. He got taken away from nursery in an ambulance. I was working overseas when I got the phone call. I ran into the nearest toilet and was physically sick. I could've flown home immediately. But my husband was with him and I knew he was taken care of. So I stayed. I had to make that decision. You get better at making those decisions.

I've had more nights than I can remember, worried sick about spiking temperatures. Then the sun rises, you dose them up on all sorts, get them off to nursery so you can put in a twelve-hour day, praying the whole time the phone doesn't ring. We used to fight over who would go and get the kids if it did. Then my husband died. I think he just figured it would be easier!

*She laughs raucously.*

M. I'm so sorry.

AGENT. Oh God no, he was right. Life is brutal. I honestly thought I was going mad in those early years. I didn't talk to anyone about it but my therapist. Which is what I would urge you to do – don't put it in your plays while you're working it all out. Don't tell them your age, don't tell them you've got kids.

M. It's all I ever really knew for certain. That I wanted kids. At school they asked us all what we wanted to do and I actually said I wanted to have a family.

AGENT. You can't say that, lovey. Not publicly. It says way too much about your class.

M. What?

AGENT. The breadth of your aspirations and ambition. People will stop expecting anything of you.

M. I think I want that.

AGENT. Believe me you don't. You'll be able to breathe for a bit, fine, but you'll soon find you're sucking air from a life full of absolute tedium. Because you let everyone assume you can't do what they want you to do, just because right now you're a bit tired.

I signed you because you were an outspoken talent.
A woman we needed to hear from. You've got the ability to articulate big, important ideas in a way other people can't. Seriously, leave the domestic issues to those that don't have that talent.

M. Right.

AGENT. I've got to run very soon was there anything else?

*M starts faffing with her bag and notebook as if she's looking for something. AGENT is trying to leave.*

M. Oh, erm, yes, let me just... what was it, erm, oh yes, that's it, I'm pregnant.

AGENT. Very good.

M. No, really, I am

My coil didn't work.

AGENT. Shit, okay, what are you going to do? Because you could probably sue somebody for that, if you

M. We're not going to sue anybody

AGENT. Well then, that's wonderful news. And you're feeling okay?

M. Brilliant. Yes. Full of, energy and, ambition.

AGENT. That's good. Our books are a real squeeze. I'm under pressure to lose anyone who's not bringing any money in.

M. I will definitely still have time to work.

AGENT. Good. Well, congratulations! Start taking the supplements.

You're a real talent, love. Don't waste it.

*A soundscape takes over: childbirth and shouting and an ambulance siren. Chaos. It fades out into the sound of a quiet room. Regular beeping can be heard from incubators just outside the door. Inside the room is the rhythmic sound of a hospital-grade breast pump and a television playing a nostalgic, classic comedy Christmas special – maybe Morecambe and Wise.*

**Scene Eight**

**A New Beginning (2)/Desolation**

M *walks awkwardly into a hospital room where* JULIE *is pumping breast milk.*

M. Hey.

JULIE. Hi.

M. How are you?

JULIE. Okay.


M. Ah, I love this. Are you watching it?

JULIE. No.

M. I'll leave it on. I'm not sure what else

JULIE. Okay.

> M *sits down with her back to* JULIE *so they are facing opposite sides of the room. The sound of another hospital grade breast pump starts up.*
>
> *Uncomfortable silence.*

M. How's Alfie?

JULIE. The doctor said he's going to die.

M. Shit.

JULIE. They've said it before. And he didn't. So.

M. Which doctor?

JULIE. Marco. He's arrogant. I've asked for a second opinion. Someone's coming from another hospital in London. Tomorrow, I think. They said that, but.

M. That's good.

JULIE. Yeah. She's an expert, in something specific, so she's going to check him over and see if they have other medication that might work. Apparently there's other medication that could work. It's really new and

M. Right. That's good.

JULIE. That's good. Isn't it.

M. You have so much milk.

JULIE. Yeah.

M. You filled a whole freezer. I mean, there's like four drawers full of yours and then mine squandering in the bottom.

JULIE. Sorry.

M. No. It's incredible.

JULIE. It won't stop coming. I keep thinking it must be a sign.

M. I wish I could make that much. It's like a drought in here.

JULIE. Probably shock.

M. Maybe.

JULIE. Not conducive to flowing lactation, they say.

M. I was the same with my first, though. Took an hour to get a drop.

JULIE. You have another?

M. Yeah, sorry. I mean. Not.

I like his little trainers. With his name on. On top of the incubator.

JULIE. His dad bought those. I haven't seen him for twelve weeks. He wants to be part of his life now.

M. I saw him.

JULIE. Sorry about that. I said he could come but I didn't think he'd be like that.

M. No, it's fine. This place gets you in a weird way.

JULIE. He's a dick, but.
  I've officially given up my job. They were getting impatient
  so I said I wasn't coming back.

M. Shit.

JULIE. They said why couldn't I work in the hours between
  ten and three and I could be back to be with him through the
  night. It's been five months now. I get it. But I can't leave
  him. How could I leave him?

M. I'm so sorry.

JULIE. How's your little one?

M. I don't really know. There are so many wires and tubes and,
  his mouth and face are just covered in plasters.

JULIE. Is he still on a ventilator?

M. Yeah. So

JULIE. They need to get him off. It'll be bad for him.

M. Right.
  I can't even tell if he's mine. If he was in a line-up, I'm not
  sure I would pick him out because looking at him is hard,
  right now. I didn't expect him to be a boy, so that was a
  big shock. And I don't know what he smells like, so. They
  asked me if I wanted to change his nappy earlier, and I don't,
  I really don't want to. I tried and he was all over the place
  and. I don't know.
  Does Alfie feel like yours?

JULIE. Yeah.

M. You are an amazing mum. Can I just say that? You really
  are. You haven't left his side for a second. And that doesn't
  mean you're not amazing if you wanted to. But you never
  leave him alone for a moment. And. I don't even know you,
  really, except for our meetings in here over the last week,
  but I just want to say, I am so proud of you. I'm sorry if
  that's. I mean, I know that's, weird. But, I really just feel
  this love for you, here, right now, this power in my chest so

overwhelming for you. I want you to know that. Because this place is intense and I would never say this, outside of these four walls, unless I was really drunk, but you are amazing.

JULIE. Thanks. I'm full.

M. Wow. Well done. Two mils for me so far. I'll stay and watch this.

JULIE. Christmas special. Should be good.

M. Yeah.

JULIE. Good luck.

M. You too.

JULIE. See you in there.

*They look at each other as if the worst thing possible is beyond the door.*

**Scene Nine**

**Weighing In/Aftershock**

*A few weeks later,* M *has taken her baby to be weighed in by the* HEALTH VISITOR. *She is unable to speak because of a massive lump in her throat.*

HV. Hello 'Mummy'. How are you? Awww. You look a little tearful. Help yourself to tissues.

It's okay to have a bad day. Pick yourself up and start again tomorrow. You sit there and I'll get him sorted.

Let's have a look at this baby then. Oh, bless him. Tiny little man.

Do you think he's gaining weight well?

Have you got your notes there?

Okay, let's have a look.

*She turns some pages.*

Here we are.

Oh wow. Right. Oh, my goodness. And they didn't pick that up on the twenty-week scan?

Gosh, what a shock, Mummy. Well, we rarely see a baby that survives this. Your little one is an absolute miracle.

You must feel very lucky.

So, you'll need to keep him isolated for as long as possible.

And I assume you know how vital it is to breastfeed. Little man needs all your milk so make that top priority.

I really think you need to see this time as a gift with your baby. Just the two of you.

Try not to think 'what if'.

Don't worry about the future.

Just live in the moment, if you can.

Get out into nature.

M. I HATE NATURE.

HV. Enjoy the fresh air. Obviously when it gets a bit warmer and stops raining. My son was up to his neck in puddles this morning. Complete rascal. There's just no tiring him out. Went to school absolutely soaked.

Oh, look at this little one. He's absolutely beautiful. You are one lucky mummy.

Shall we get him on these scales then?

## Scene Ten

## Getting Out/No Escape

M *is trying to get her four-year-old daughter ready for nursery while the baby cries. Her* DAUGHTER *is watching a YouTube video about pregnant Barbie dolls.*

M. Come on, get ready.

DAUGHTER. I'm tired.

M. We're late. What is this?

DAUGHTER. Pregnant Barbies, good and evil, look, that one's had a baby and they've made it a crib out of a barbecue, and she wears that bikini cos it's hot as hell in there. What is hell?

M. It's where the devil lives.

DAUGHTER. You said I'm the devil. In car eight.

M. Incarnate. Turn it off.

DAUGHTER. I love it.

M. YouTube is banned. Get dressed.

DAUGHTER. I am dressed.

M. Out of your pyjamas. Please.

DAUGHTER. There's nothing to wear.

M. Why?

DAUGHTER. Because you didn't wash anything.

M. Oh. Shit. Ships.

DAUGHTER. Where?

M. On the sea. Generally. Just change your top. You've got all stuff round your mouth.

DAUGHTER. Nutella.

M. Who gave you that?

DAUGHTER. I got it while you were looking at your phone.

M. You climbed up on the stool?

DAUGHTER. You're so grumpy. You should get out more. That's what Granny said.

M. Get. Dressed. Turn. That. Off.

DAUGHTER. Mum.

M. What?

DAUGHTER. Yesterday we did this thing where Miss Natalie taught us what to do if a naughty dog gets into nursery.

M. Right?

DAUGHTER. It was so funny. There's this really loud alarm, and we have to get down under the tables and curl up and stay perfectly still and quiet. Miss Natalie locks all the doors and we have to keep down below any windows so the naughty dog can't see us.

M. You had to hide under the tables?

DAUGHTER. It's called a drill. Naughty dog drill. Only I don't understand how it's a drill because there are no screws or nails or anything else.

M. Right.

DAUGHTER. I'm ready.

M. Let's not bother today.

DAUGHTER. I want to go. I want to do the naughty dog drill again.

M. You're too tired.

DAUGHTER. I'm not now.

M. Let's stay here, lock the doors, close all the curtains and snuggle down. We could watch a movie.

DAUGHTER. Can I watch pregnant Barbies?

M. Yes.

**Scene Eleven**

**Socialising/Public Malfunction**

M *is at toddler group. She can't keep her eyes off her son.*

EM. Which one's yours?

M. Lying there, in the green hoody, with the fence around him.

EM. Oh, adorable. Hang on, we were pregnant at the same time.

M. Yeah, he's just, small. Complications, so

EM. Oh bless you. Small but perfectly formed.

M. Not exactly.

EM. That one's mine. Hugo. Absolute menace. Launching himself into the ball pit. Little action man. He was walking at eight months.

M. Wow.

EM. Bless you. Must've been so scary. Did they say why it happened?

M. No one knows exactly.

EM. Well, you mustn't blame yourself.

M. Thanks.

EM. I mean, you were always so active in pregnancy, weren't you? I was in absolute awe of how much you did. I was just there, taking all the advice, and you were off to London to do your projects and I just thought 'wow'. I used to be in London A LOT by the way, many lives ago!

M. Right.

EM. Know it *really* well. It's so polluted though, isn't it? I mean it's bad enough here but London. That kid in the news actually died of smog.

M. Awful.

EM. It was what you had to do at the time so you must not blame yourself.

Are you weaning yet?

M. Kind of.

EM. So, we started with sweet potato and then we followed up with pretty much every vegetable we could find on Oc-A-do. He just ate it all up no problem, at all. But, then: Oh. My. God...

M. What?

EM. My mum gave him a Lindt Lindor.

M. Right.

EM. I could've killed her. He hadn't even laid eyes on chocolate before, now it's like he won't eat anything else. I've found these cacao and avocado balls that might just fool him for a bit longer.

M. Fingers crossed.

EM. Although, hang on, I do have a hilarious video of him tasting chocolate for the first time. Wait one second. (*She is scrolling through her videos*.) God, the weaning off the breast is causing absolute havoc with my dreams. Do you find that? Any crazy dreams?

M. Yeah. Last night, I had this dream about my old Art teacher – we were fucking in this cage. He just pushed me up against the bars and my fat is squeezing through like raw pork and I'm wearing nothing but a shoe lace.

EM. Sorry, I was looking through these, what did you say?

M. Not really a dreamer.

EM. Well, we're all different. Did you do baby-led?

M. What?

EM. Weaning?

EM *follows* M*'s gaze and sees* JOE.

Oh, hi.

M. Hello.

JOE. Hi, I'm Joe

M. M

EM. Em

JOE. That's easy.

EM. Which one's yours?

JOE. Camille. With the little bow. My wife makes them. She's got an Etsy store. Bow Belles?

EM. Mummy to boys here! Aww, she's a beauty.

JOE. Yeah. Thank goodness. Keeps us awake all night. Very lucky she's cute.

M. Yeah, cos if she was ugly, you'd probably like smash her head into the door frame, or, whatever

JOE *looks at* M *like she's an utter weirdo.*

Sorry, I thought that's what you were implying.

JOE. I wasn't implying anything.

M. Right, God, sorry.

So, what did you mean? Lucky she's cute?

JOE. Just, it helps, when I'm, shattered, yknow?

M. That she's aesthetically pleasing. Got you.

EM. She's a writer. She's a bit... Mine's Hugo in the Frugi. And hers is

M. That one.

JOE. How old?

M. One.

EM. Thirteen months.

JOE. Wow. He's

EM. Tiny!

M. Yeah.

EM. He was really ill when he was born.

JOE. Ah, I'm sorry about that. Must've been tough.

M. Yeah. He died, really, and was resuscitated. I watched them stick needles into his head, and they punctured his skin all over to try and find veins that apparently weren't straight enough, and he had to have an operation and they were ventilating him, and the tube was actually bigger than his windpipe. So that

JOE. But he's doing so well now, he looks so robust.

M. Tiny.

JOE. Yeah, but solid, you know? Little fighter.

EM. Little itty-bitty champion.

M. Yeah, he chokes a lot, and, yeah, I mean, then there's life to deal with, on top of all that, and

JOE. Totally. I always say to my wife, I am so grateful Camille's normal. But you're just so lucky he's here. I guess you really focus on that, right?

EM. It's not good to dwell.

JOE. I mean, gratitude is something you really learn about as a parent.

EM. Totally. Whoops, Hugo's throwing balls at that little girl's head. He is *so* like his daddy, such a flirt! Back in a mo.

*Awkward silence.*

M. I should tell you I have varicose veins and broken capillaries, all over my legs, like all over, I should say that now. Not due to motherhood or anything. I've just, always had them.

JOE. Okay.

M. Just, in case, we are going to

JOE. What?

M. No, I mean, you're the only man here and it's like a massive neon Vegas sign in my head is just flashing and blasting,

like 'Arrgh, Arrrgh, Arrrgh, Arrrgh', man alert, man in the
territory

JOE. Right

M. I wish I'd've worn make-up, to be honest, as soon as I saw
you I was like 'Fuck! Fuck it. FUCK. IT. Man in the room.'
I assumed you were gay but then I heard you talking about
your wife and I was like, 'Why, the fuck, didn't I wash?'
I mean, yes, that is egg, from last week, and yes, my trousers
smell slightly, more than slightly, of leaked piss and, arrrgh,
why didn't you call ahead?

JOE. You're fine.

M. I look like this, all the time, so it's no surprises. I wouldn't
want to get into anything

JOE. Get into anything?

M. Whatever the lingo is these days. I wouldn't want to do it
in full make-up and then let you down later with this, look.
Because we're bound to bump into each other, afterwards, at
some point.

JOE. Right, well, anyway, I'm just going to

M. Going to

JOE. Go over there to talk to Pamela about weaning

M. No, sorry, stay, it's

JOE. I'm married. Bow Belles?

M. I'm married. Course. No. I'm married. Weaning is a piece of
piss, it's like, buy some jars, take a spoon. Weaned.

Give them some steamed carrot batons if you want to look
like you made an effort. Mash up a banana at the table.

JOE. Thanks.

M. Except, be careful cos bananas have these stringy bits that
look like little worms in their poo and it can be a bit of a
shock.

Joe, sorry, If we do, ever, get into something, don't think about little banana worms in poo when you're, down there, or, whatever. Sorry. I mean.

JOE. Okay. I'm going to leave.

M. It was great meeting you. Joe. Great.

## Scene Twelve

### Me-Time/Self-Disgust

M *is alone and talking aloud – maybe through a megaphone because she's just desperate to bust out of herself.*

M. Things I do when my kids aren't here:

Pile filthy pots in the sink.
Write 'to do' lists I'll never look at again.
Binge re-runs of *Catfish*.
Eat multiple grab-bags of anything.
Watch porn with the sound on.
Google pictures of diseases.

Fuck. This. List. Is. Dull.

## Scene Thirteen

### Try Paracetamol/Saving Myself

M *goes to see the* DOCTOR.

DOCTOR. What seems to be the problem?

M. I've got all these cramps and stomach pains. I feel awful.
    I don't know if I need tests or?

DOCTOR. It's probably your cycle, it's to be expected. Have you tried paracetamol?

M. I have.

DOCTOR. Did it help?

M. No.

And. Okay. Well, this is, embarrassing, because you're a, man, basically, and possibly, on some level, thinking about... anyway... my poo comes suddenly and I can't stop it. The other day I pooed myself because I couldn't open my front door in time.

DOCTOR. You've had children, everything has dropped inside of you, muscles are weaker. Do you do your pelvic floors?

M. I feel like that horse has bolted. Except the horse is poo.

DOCTOR. Okay. Well, you need to help yourself and do your pelvic floors. Give up alcohol and coffee, eat more fruit and vegetables, keep a food diary and come back in three months.

M. Okay.

Thank you.

I just

DOCTOR. We've only got five minutes. If you need a double appointment you'll have to rebook.

M. I just get to this point where I want to escape my life. I hate everything in my life and I want to escape it.

DOCTOR. You want to escape your life?

M. Yes.

DOCTOR. So, are you saying

M. I'm not going to kill myself. I just mean every month, for at least a week, I hate my life, I hate my kids, I hate my husband, I can't work, but I can't tell them I can't work so I just cry a lot and drag myself around. I am frozen for a week, maybe two, and then it lifts and I'm a sort of super, 1970s hippy version of myself, walking along at sunset feeling full of love for the planet and myself and my fellow humans. For, like, a day.

DOCTOR. Okay. Yes. That sounds normal.

M. But mainly I'm just scared. All the time.

DOCTOR. Of what?

M. That they will die. I don't know what to do about that particular thing.

DOCTOR. Okay, so what do you want today? Antidepressants?

M. I don't know. I think I want you to tell me, in your professional opinion, that it will be okay.


DOCTOR. What are your pastimes?

M. I can't really remember. Yoga?

DOCTOR. Really?

M. No.

DOCTOR. What defines you? What makes you who you are?

M. I don't know. Writing. I'm a writer. Kind of.

DOCTOR. And how much writing have you been doing?

M. None.

DOCTOR. Why not?

M. I'm just a bit busy. And numb.

DOCTOR. What does writing mean to you?

M. I don't know. Failure. Trying to catch smoke and pin it to something. Cutting my arm open with a school compass and letting the blood. It's like being buried in a coffin deep in the ground but somehow having a pipeline up through the earth and a megaphone on the end of it.

DOCTOR. Maybe write a letter to yourself. See what comes. My great aunt was a writer.

M. Really?

DOCTOR. Yes, Constance McKay, rather prolific.

M. Did she have children?

DOCTOR. No.

M. Oh.

DOCTOR. She wanted them. But she was never blessed in that way. She wrote about it. Which was very courageous for the day. Although those essays were never published. Still I think her writing healed her somewhat. Might be worth a try.

If I may...

M. Yes.

DOCTOR. In my professional opinion, if I may, I think you should write, fuck, sweat, dance, inhabit all of your talents in any way possible, share them unashamedly with the world. Help us quarrel with what it is to be human. That will perhaps, in turn, help *you* to breathe.

M. Right.

Did you really say that?

DOCTOR. Of course not. We had five minutes and three hundred people in the waiting room.

But I might have got to it, if we'd had time. Possibly. I'm not a machine.

M. No. Thanks, doctor.

DOCTOR. I do really care about women's issues. Believe it or not. I've got daughters.

M. Right.

DOCTOR. I hope it helps.

**Scene Fourteen**

**Letting the Blood/I Want My Mum**

M *is writing at home. Her* MUM *has taken the baby out, but comes back earlier than agreed.*

MUM. We're back

M. Bloody hell, Mum!
I thought you'd be longer.

MUM. He's fast asleep so I thought you might as well have him here.

M. What if he wakes up?

MUM. I've got so much to do.

M. Like what?

MUM. How's the writing going?

M. Okay. I've got a headache

MUM. You've always got a headache

M. Have I?

MUM. Seems like it. You should stretch more. And stand up straight. Pretend there's a string through your back. Holding you up. It's all that hunching over your phone. I do yoga. At the gym.

M. Well done.

MUM. You can do it on your TV now. In your house.

M. My carpet stinks.

MUM. Well, clean it then. Honestly.

M. What?

MUM. When he's napping, seize your chance and do one task.

M. I'm knackered.

MUM. It's a state of mind. Put some make-up on. You need to get out more.

M. It's raining.

MUM. Not all the time.

Your bin's full, shall I put it out?

M. You're alright.

MUM. I don't mind.

M. Leave it.

MUM. That smell must be bothering you.

M. It's fine. I'll do it.

MUM. What are you writing?


M. Can I read it to you?

MUM. Of course.

M. Don't say anything stupid.

MUM. As if I would.

M. Seriously. I just want to hear it out loud.

MUM. Is it for that big theatre?

M. No, it's just

MUM. Oh, I thought you meant paid work.

M. Don't bother.

MUM. No. Come on.

I promise.

M *reads*.

M. Dear M,

It's a letter to myself

MUM. Right.

M. Dear M,

As I write this, I am thinking about all the versions of you. The happy toddler in her grandma's papery arms, the fat little translucent girl with the severe fringe and the foul mouth, the self-hating teenager who had sex with her clothes on.

You wanted children. Always. It wasn't a question of if but when. Still you waited until you were old, by the averages of the past. Too busy walking breathless around art galleries with alcohol increasing your ideas of possibility, increasing your ideas of who you might be. Sometimes you panic that you won't know your children for long enough because you waited.

You prepared for a home birth. Your mum was against it. Hospital, she said. You must be mad, she said. Still, you talked your husband into it. Stupid.

And it wasn't what you expected. The midwives left you at the wrong point and you pretty much delivered alone. You held onto the baby in the birth canal and when they finally ran in and started screaming at you, you were shocked and scared and sort of frozen. You almost killed him. You are not enough.

The baby was snuffly, they said he might be so not to worry. And then your daughter came home to meet him and you gave her the silver shoes she wanted, glittery 'clockers', wrapped in paper, and you told her they were a present from her hours-old brother. That he picked them out. She didn't ask how.

You agreed with your husband to take it in turns to keep watch for an hour at a time. Because the baby was still snuffly and something wasn't right but it was Christmas Eve and Santa was coming and you so wanted it to be okay.

And if it isn't okay, you don't really know what to do about it. You are devastatingly tired. And you're thinking 'Why did we do this? Why did we explode our life with another?'

In the morning your regular midwife comes while your daughter's opening her presents and you quietly say 'I think his breathing is a bit weird' and she takes one look and says 'Yes, we'd better get an ambulance'.

You're hovering around and she tells you to get ready. You're wearing the night shirt you gave birth in. You want to wear it because it smells like birth and you're not ready to shed that skin yet. You haven't bathed. You're aching and swollen and your face looks like a red beach ball. You run upstairs and tie a gold scarf around your head. Like putting a frilly bonnet on a pig. It's Christmas Day. You always dress up on Christmas Day. And your mum is smiling and holding this oven dish of breakfast and she doesn't understand what's happening. She thinks you'll be back for lunch.

And then in the hospital he dies in your arms. People in cheap Christmas jumpers with tinsel round their necks tear him from you and manipulate his tiny body on a big cold resuscitation table while ten other humans, who are not you, work tirelessly to keep him alive. You are not enough because you can't keep him alive. They are asking you to make decisions, decisions that will alter the course of this boy's life. He is an abstract thing still. A fully formed human but you don't know him yet and he hasn't spoken or showed you he loves you, really, except you know he needs you. They say he needs you. This horrible, veiny, indecisive, impractical, forgetful girl in the gold headscarf who last night was wondering why she'd decided to have another child. He needs you. Wow. Why?

Two unforgettable weeks on the ward, with mothers suffering and babies dying and procedures and surprises and nightmares and swollen legs and vaginal checks and milking and hot, hot, hot rooms and cracked feet and pale-orange walls and methodical milk freezing and queuing up for dinner and visits from our daughter who is having Christmas without us. I am not enough because I'm glad she's having Christmas without us. But I miss her and I want her, just her, although I whisper to a god, if there is one, that I will do anything to see the baby survive and thrive. Except die because my daughter needs me. But I will do anything else. And die, if I have to.

And eventually we get out alive, which no one was expecting, and we live in the bedroom at home for a few days because I forget I can carry him outside of the door. And slowly, so slowly...

That's all I've got so far.

MUM. Right.

M. What?

MUM. It's quite long.

M. Yeah. I'll probably delete it.

Mum.

MUM. What?

M. When you tell me to put make-up on, or try to empty my bin, it makes me feel, disgusting. And I already feel disgusting. I think I just need you, out of everyone, to make me feel like I'm, good.

MUM. Okay.

**Scene Fifteen**

**Tribes/The Deepest Truths**

M *is alone in a coffee shop.* JULIE *enters. She is looking for* M *but doesn't recognise her.*

M. Hi, Julie

JULIE. Oh hi. Sorry. You look different.

M. Not in my pyjamas with my boobs out?

JULIE. Something like that.

M. You look great. How are you?

JULIE. I'm okay. How are you?

M. Fine. Yeah.

JULIE. Where's, the little one?

M. He's with my mum today.

JULIE. Oh, right. You could have. I thought he'd

M. No. I know. I thought it would be easier, you know. Nice to get out and. How are you?

JULIE. Are you eating, or?

M. I thought I might just get a pastry or, we can eat, off the menu if you want or, whatever

JULIE. Are you still breastfeeding?

M. Erm, a bit, trying to

JULIE. Okay, so you need a meal

M. It's fine.

JULIE. No. Come on, let's eat. I'll get the lasagne.

M. I'll get the same, then.

JULIE. So how is

M. Yeah, he's okay. He's weak, really, but, he's doing good, and

JULIE. Yeah. Are you coping okay?

M. I'm okay. I mean, it's difficult.

JULIE. Of course.

M. How are you?

JULIE. And is he, getting stronger or?

M. It takes a lot to feed him. He chokes a lot and it's. Anyway. Sorry. How are you? Really?

JULIE. Yeah. Every day's different.

M. Are you still with Alfie's dad?

JULIE. I am.

M. That's good.

JULIE. I don't know. I mean, he's the last thing I've got that

M. Of course.

JULIE. I got a new job. A few months ago now

M. Wow. That's. Amazing.

JULIE. I started at a new salon.

M. And how is it?

JULIE. I have to pretend that none of this happened and
talk to people about *Love Island* and *Bake Off* and Prince
Harry. (*Change these references to reflect the time of the
production.*)

M. Yeah.

JULIE. It's okay. It helps sometimes.

M. That's good.

JULIE. And I'm so exhausted that I sleep.

M. That's good.

JULIE. Yeah.

M (*about the staff*). Where are they?

JULIE. I don't know.

M. I'll go to the bar and order.

JULIE. Do you mind if I don't?

M. What?

JULIE. Order.

M. Yeah. I mean no.

JULIE. I thought this would be okay but

M. It's not

JULIE. No.

M. Right.

JULIE. No one in there went through the same thing, I get that. But your tribe are the ones that lived, and mine are probably those that didn't

M. Right.

JULIE. I'm really sorry. I didn't think I'd be

M. Of course. I'm sorry.

JULIE. I don't want you to be sorry. But all I can think of is your little boy at home. And I wouldn't have left mine behind to meet you.

M. Right.

JULIE. So, let's leave it.

M. Okay.

JULIE. Have a very happy life. I wish you everything. Honestly.

M. You too.

JULIE. It's too late for me.

M. No. There's other stuff.

JULIE. Yeah, there's other stuff.

M. Definitely.

**Scene Sixteen**

**Practical Ways To Survive/Tiny Air Holes After Asphyxiation**

M *is sitting on the bed.* HUSBAND *tiptoes in.*

HUSBAND. They're asleep, thank fuck.

M. I think we should co-parent

HUSBAND. What?

M. I've seen a thing lately, a trend, where people are saying it's better to have lots of different partners, short and sweet, that don't drain your emotional energy. So, you have their body and their chat, but you have the capacity to put your energy and emotions into the kids and the work.

HUSBAND. Are you serious?

M. Yeah.

HUSBAND. So, you think lots of short-term partners will need less emotional investment than me? How much do you think I get?

M. I really believe co-parenting will be better. It'll give us both the chance to think. Have our own space. Take care of the kids properly, with energy. Feel alive again. We're both decent people. We can do this well.

HUSBAND. You're actually, serious?

M. I see people co-parenting on Instagram. They basically spend every other weekend in Airbnbs around the world reading massive books. It's a no-brainer. Why are we trying to make this work?

HUSBAND. This does work.

M. It doesn't because you want sex and I can't. I don't know how to do marital sex. It's alien. In my formative years there were no open examples of marital sex.

HUSBAND. Sting and Trudie.

M. Tantric. Sure. Who can be bothered with that?

HUSBAND. People who co-parent, maybe.

M. Exactly.

HUSBAND. I think you've got a rose-tinted view of this.

M. People say 'Why the fuck are we still asking public women how they juggle family life and professional life'? And I get it. I do. Men don't get asked that question. But deep down I'm thinking, 'Please ask them. Ask every last one of them, because I need to know. Ask them more. Ask them: 'Do you actually have sex and do all this other stuff?' and 'Are you physically worried sick about your kids every second?' and 'Aren't you fucking wrung-out exhausted and on the floor?' Ask more, because I need to know how everyone else is doing this shit and making it look possible.

HUSBAND. You've been through a trauma. It's okay to stall.

M. For how long? It's been literally years. No, I think co-parenting is the answer. On your nights I can stay up till daybreak and drink and write and be myself. People I worked with years ago, they're getting BAFTAs and film commissions. And I think, fine, I've got time, their journey is not my journey. But before we know it, our kids are going to be achieving the things we always wanted for ourselves and we'll be wondering what the fuck happened.

HUSBAND. So, this is the end of our marriage?

M. Possibly.

HUSBAND. Possibly? Right.

M. Look, I know it's heartbreaking and all that but I seriously don't have the energy to think about it right now.

HUSBAND. Good for you.

M. Yeah.

Say something.

HUSBAND. Like what?

M. I don't know. Something.

HUSBAND. Words are easy for you. Like shovelling the little spade into the pick 'n' mix.

M. Sorry, what?

HUSBAND. Like no care, just shove it in and see what comes out, what spills, what lands in the bag

M. What is this weird analogy?

HUSBAND. Words are your currency, or whatever, and for some reason that makes you feel superior. I used to be amazed by it, the way you could just spew words and say how you feel. But it doesn't put you above the rest of us. Just because you can articulate stuff. The rest of us, working away, quietly putting our back into it, showing up every day.

M. I am showing up. Fuck me. I've spent my life showing up. Just because you're a man you want a medal for showing up

I've been showing up! I show up

HUSBAND. Yeah, and screaming about it. Like a fucking machine gun.

M. What?

HUSBAND. We weren't all brought up in noisy houses with people swearing and screaming and throwing plant pots at each other

M. That was once

HUSBAND. We weren't all naked and shitting and showering together and told to speak our minds or explain our emotions or say I love you at the end of every fucking sentence. We weren't all harmonising 'Happy Birthday'. Some of us were quiet. Some of us got on with things. Some of us put our emotions into the outdoors or gardening or swimming or whatever.

M. You're so wholesome.

HUSBAND. Shouting was showing off. Attention seeking. It's hard to unlearn that. I want to. I have stuff to say.

M. Do you?

HUSBAND. Of course I do. I'm not some fucking automated service. But it takes me so long to form a sentence, by the time I do, you've written the fucking book on it.

M. I wish.

HUSBAND. I could scream this fucking house down with things I want to say.

M. Go on then!

HUSBAND. I don't trust myself to say it right. And then it's out there, all wrong, and it cuts you.

M. Just say it! For God's sake. Or else what's the point in any of this?

HUSBAND. Okay.

You have never made me feel safe.

I never knew what was going on inside your head. I used to like it. But right now…

I didn't expect him to see his first birthday. I'm scared too. But you expect me to just, suck it up. Because it's not attractive. Be honest, it's not. And God knows I don't need anything else about me to gross you out. But now, actually, I think, with all this, other noise, now, I really just need you to make me feel safe. I need you to really fucking love me. Because it's scary.

You're lucky. You are so lucky to be able to write yourself into another life.

M. But /

HUSBAND. / I know it's not easy. I know it's hard to heave words out when you're not in the mood or whatever, but at the end of it all you have this ability to escape. You can go somewhere else inside yourself. But me? This is my world. This is where I'm trapped.

M. Trapped?

HUSBAND. Yeah.

And, and, sex, is the only time I feel like, like, that I can escape. It's like this other bit of me, this trapped, shit-scared bit of me, gets to come out and, I don't know, breathe, or, let go, or something.

Fuck.

I don't know how else to do that.

*Pause.*

If you want me to go, or you want to go, we'll have to deal with that. But I think maybe you will miss the safety of this. I could be wrong. I could be completely wrong. Maybe that's marriage. Constantly questioning whether it still makes sense. It's not what either of us expected.

M. Isn't it?

HUSBAND. You expected this?

M. I didn't really think that much about it. I think I always imagine marriage is only movie length. What happens after the end?

HUSBAND. A lot of kindness, probably. Some sex, hopefully.

M. Sounds exhausting.

HUSBAND. Definitely. It's why people give up on dreams. You can't do it all.

M. You want me to give up on my dreams?

HUSBAND. I don't think so.

M. So, what do you want me to do?

HUSBAND. I want you to realise that all this time I've been here, making sure you're okay. I need you to at least recognise that. Because I feel like I'm never part of the story. It's like you're always looking around getting ready to jump.

M. I'm afraid I'll wake up in ten years and realise this is all I am. And I'm afraid of waking up in ten years to find I've messed this up. They told me I could be anything. It's bollocks. I didn't fully grasp, that when I chose this, other roads would be blocked. I'll never pad barefoot around my New York City apartment, looking out at the skyline while I write my next movie. That was one hazy idea I had for myself. But I guess the roots I had here, my own family, lasting love, all that just pulled harder.

HUSBAND. And now you regret it?

M. I suppose I just wonder if it was always going to be like this. The way I was raised, the films I watched, the music I listened to. Like when you see sausages in an advert and then all day you want sausages. Maybe that's me, but the sausages are my destiny. What part of this did I really choose? Did any of us choose?

HUSBAND. So, if you could completely wipe your brain and start again, what would you do?

M. I don't know. I imagine that New York apartment, and I'm there all shaved and moisturised in silk shorts and cami, pen holding my hair up, Macbook open on the bed – and suddenly I realise that's just *Sex and the City*. So, I take Carrie out and put myself there instead and I'm trying to write a film, the studio needs a draft, the draft is awful, I'm depressed, unwashed, I want to die. And I really just want to lie in bed with my babies. Only they don't exist in that skyline apartment.

I don't know if I ever saw a scenario that really suited me. That I felt could actually be real for me. It's like when I try to imagine who else I might be married to, and I can't.

HUSBAND. That's the nicest thing you've ever said to me.

M. I'm disappointed in myself.

HUSBAND. Why?

M. Because even the conclusion of all this is so provincial. It's not even a conclusion. It's exhaustion. And defeat. And inevitability.

HUSBAND. Maybe that's just what real life looks like.

M. Nice.

HUSBAND. Maybe you're just too tired and scared right now to imagine how the New York thing could work. Give it another few years. Everything changes.

M. We're never going to live in New York. You hate cities.

HUSBAND. That is true.


M. In the hospital, when I was completely hollowed out, you made me feel safe. Thank you.


HUSBAND. So, are we co-parenting then or what?

M. I don't know. I'll sleep on it.

HUSBAND. Maybe check Instagram, see what they say.

M. Fuck off. But yeah, I probably will.

*They turn out the light. Darkness. A strange baby voice shouts 'MAMA. MAMA.'*

I'll go.

M *starts to walk across the stage to a cot. Ominous music creeps in. A red light washes over the baby's bedroom.* M *goes to the cot and looks in but it's empty.*

Baby?!

*She is starting to panic.*

Baby, where are you?

*She notices the baby is in the corner of the room, watching her.*

Oh, thank God, sweetheart, you're there. How did you get out of your cot?

Baby? What's wrong? Your eyes are all red.

*A possessed voice comes from the baby.*

BABY. Shhhhhhh.

M. Oh my God.

BABY. Listen to me and stay quiet. There is going to be a murder. I've seen it.

M. What? Who are you? Where's my baby?

BABY. It's me, Mama. I have seen a murder. It hasn't happened yet. But it will. You have to go to the police.

M. They'll never believe me.

BABY. Make them believe you. Or people will die.

M. What people?

HUSBAND (*from the other room*). M! You okay?

M. Yeah.

HUSBAND. Come to bed.

M. Just a minute.

BABY. You must call the police and tell them what I saw. I'm afraid. Only you can /

M. Oh shush

*An abrupt lighting change.*

## Scene Seventeen

## An Ending/A New Beginning (3)

M *is in a meeting with* JOSH. *Jake's seat is empty.*

JOSH. Okay, so Jake and I have read the latest draft. Thanks so much for sharing that.

It's still not the baby who has premonitions, which is obviously what we suggested all those years ago.

M. I tried, but it wasn't really working. I did add a song.

JOSH. You did. One.

M. I don't think this is a musical.

JOSH. I tell you what. Let's chat about what we do have and we'll take it from there. How does that sound?

M. Great.

JOSH. Do you want to start? Or shall I just

M. You go.

JOSH. OK, I guess our first question was, what is the play really about, from your perspective?

M. I think, lots of people say nice things about mothers – grand statements like 'Oh they're shaping civilisation'. But I think, if we're honest, underneath it all there's this deeply ingrained, low-level disgust.

JOSH. Disgust?

M. Yeah. Like women who choose to have kids should just shut up and get on with it.

JOSH. And what about women who choose not to have kids. Does society look favourably upon them?

M. No.

JOSH. Okay.

Let's look at some of the scenes. The man on the market stall? Remind me, what's that actually about?

M. I suppose he represents people who assume her potential can't be fulfilled now she's gone and got a kid. And obviously her own self-loathing.

JOSH. But still, you have sex with him.

M. *She* has sex with him. Yes.

JOSH. Don't you think it would be more powerful if he wants it and she walks away?

M. No.

JOSH. Why not?

M. Because no matter how civilised we hope we've become, sadly some of us still really want dickheads to like us. Until we manage to unpick ourselves out of that, I guess.

JOSH. Right, so, do you have any thoughts on your protagonist?

M. Of course.

JOSH. Okay, so in the scene with her husband, he's just had sex with her when she didn't want it. And then they mention briefly that he's watched a porn video called 'stepdaughter and stepdad' or something horrific. He can't come back from that. And if she's married to him, and continues to be, then she is either a victim or part of the problem.

M. She's probably a bit of both. It's complicated, isn't it?

JOSH. But an audience will never be able to sympathise with him after that. We don't want them to!

M. What do you mean by an audience?

JOSH. Touché.

M. No, genuine question.

JOSH. I can see this play has made you very vocal. No, I mean, it's great.

Look, the thing is, as a piece of drama, I don't really get where you're coming from.

M. Yeah, I understand that.

JOSH. You do?

M. I think, what we really need here, is someone who can facilitate this discussion in a way that will help me say what I need to say. Who gets me. Who can be the best sort of midwife for my instincts.

JOSH. You mean a woman?

M. Probably. I think I've got something to say. But I need to be vulnerable and open and honest and trip over my words and say sorry and thank you and mess things up without you assuming I'm just a scatter-brained girl who can't deliver.

Maybe it's me. I'm not ruling that out. At my school it was a crime to be clever. It makes it hard to come in here and own my voice and defend things that you will never understand. I might need help with that sometimes, shameful as it is.

JOSH. I mean, some of the stuff you wrote in there was really interesting.

M. Interesting like 'written by a man' interesting?

JOSH. Come on. That's not fair. We invited you here because we were excited by your work. We thought you could write for a big stage. We backed you. We just wanted you to be ambitious.

M. I'm trying to tell the truth. I'm trying to connect with other women who will see themselves here. Who currently feel buried alive. I think that is ambitious.

I get it. I do. Men don't want to watch a play by a woman about being a woman because they have no idea how it feels – they've never needed to.

But I have to say this stuff. And I don't want to dress it up as a horror or a thriller.

JOSH. Why not? Attack from the inside. Write about motherhood but disguise it as something more compelling. In the three act structure, like you did in *Riot*.

M. I don't want to write it in the three-act structure. I want to use the menstrual cycle as a structure. With its constant peaks and dips and optimism and rage, and this fragile fluctuating sense of self - that half of us are constructing our existence around already, by the way. I want to heave my guts up and give them to the world in any structure I like. I think I'm just going to write it.

JOSH. Look, we're under a lot of pressure here. It's been a few years, since our first meeting, and Jake and I have

M. Where is Jake?

JOSH. He's in a meeting.

M. Who with?

JOSH. An emerging writer.

M. Right. Great.

*She stands to leave.*

JOSH. That's it?

M. I think so, isn't it?

I'm sorry I couldn't be what you wanted.

*Hopeful music starts to play (Think 'She's Like a Rainbow by The Rolling Stones') – building as the scene comes to an end.*

JOSH. Where're you off to now?

M. I have to take care of my kids.

JOSH. Agggh, you've still got them?

M. Yep. Still got them. They're tied to a street lamp just outside.

JOSH. God bless 'em. Give 'em a squeeze from us.

M. I will.

JOSH. And if you ever write another *Riot*, we want to be the first to read it.

*The music grows louder and louder. M leaves the meeting with a renewed spring in her step. Outside it is raining. Two small children are tied to the lamp post. She dances over to them, unties them, picks them up and swings them around laughing and smiling. She dances in the rain as the music plays, triumphant and rousingly loud. This could be interrupted by her first review. Maybe she takes out her phone and sees it. Maybe it's on a newspaper stand outside and she picks up the broadsheet. Maybe it's a voiceover that she doesn't hear. Maybe she lip-synchs it.*

### Broadsheet review, one star, Jonathan Darcy

A pram in the hallway has long been seen as creative suicide and (*the*) *woman* is the latest product of a flailing mother with too little time on her hands. After the loud but questionable success of *Riot*, all eyes were on the latest offering from this regional writer. But some of the fighting spirit seems to have been bled dry from this promising, not-so-youthful talent by sleepless nights, a ripped-up cunt and two kids. What a shame. With little to no recognisable structure, simplified gender politics and a basic appraisal of men as either sexually regressive or patronisingly ignorant, the play bleats about the exhaustion suffered by this particular woman without giving airtime to the strides we have made as a society since Pankhurst starved herself silly. No doubt desperate women on various social media platforms will sound the claxon of solidarity with empty phrases such as 'hard relate'. Relate as they will, they wouldn't know structure if it smothered them on a quiet street. Let's hope for more substance once the little ones can wipe their own arses and watch TV uninterrupted for a few sweet years. Otherwise, make way for the next playwright with potential. They're as common as Cornflakes, dear. What a disappointment. And to think we once thought she might have been interesting.

**A Nick Hern Book**

(*the*) *Woman* first published in Great Britain as a paperback original in 2025 by Nick Hern Books Limited, The Glasshouse, 49a Goldhawk Road, London W12 8QP, in association with New Perspectives and Royal & Derngate, Northampton

(*the*) *Woman* copyright © 2025 Jane Upton

Jane Upton has asserted her right to be identified as the author of this work

Designed and typeset by Nick Hern Books, London
Printed in Great Britain by Mimeo Ltd, Huntingdon, Cambridgeshire PE29 6XX

A CIP catalogue record for this book is available from the British Library

ISBN 978 1 83904 445 8

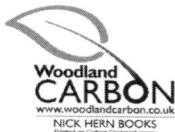

www.nickhernbooks.co.uk/environmental-policy

Nick Hern Books' authorised representative in the EU is
Easy Access System Europe – Mustamäe tee 50, 10621 Tallinn, Estonia
*email* gpsr.requests@easproject.com